P9-DGY-787

TRANSFORMING RUSSIA

BOOKS BY JOHN R. ROBERSON

China: From Manchu to Mao

Japan: From Shogun to Sony

ATHENEUM   1992   New York

MAXWELL MACMILLAN CANADA
Toronto

MAXWELL MACMILLAN INTERNATIONAL
New York   Oxford   Singapore   Sydney

TRANSFORMING
ℜUSSIA

1682 TO 1991

JOHN R. ROBERSON

Copyright © 1992 by John R. Roberson

ATHENEUM
Macmillan Publishing Company
866 Third Avenue
New York, NY 10022

Maxwell Macmillan Canada, Inc.
1200 Eglinton Avenue East
Suite 200
Don Mills, Ontario M3C 3N1

Macmillan Publishing Company is part of the Maxwell Communication Group of Companies.

Library of Congress Cataloging-in-Publication Data
Roberson, John R.
Transforming Russia: 1682 to 1991 / by John R. Roberson.—1st ed.
p.   cm.
Includes bibliographical references.
Summary: Traces the history of Russia from the late seventeenth-early eighteenth century reign of Peter the Great through the establishment of a new republic in 1991.
ISBN 0–689–31495–7
1. Soviet Union—History—1689–1800—Juvenile literature.
2. Soviet Union—History—19th century—Juvenile literature.
3. Soviet Union—History—20th century—Juvenile literature.
[1. Soviet Union—History]   I. Title.
DK127.R59   1992
947—dc20   92–1377

First edition
Printed in the United States of America
10 9 8 7 6 5 4 3 2 1
Book design by Black Angus Design Group

To Charlene, my dear wife and helpmate

ACKNOWLEDGMENTS

First I would like to express my gratitude to Fedor de Nikanov of New York, my mentor and friend, and my most direct link to Imperial Russia. An objet d'art he gave me twenty-five years ago still stands faithfully by my keyboard today. Then to Jeanne Williams of Portal, Arizona, whose research in Russia immediately preceded ours, and who generously shared with us contacts, maps, guides, and lessons learned as we made our preparations.

The New York Public Library's Research Library and Mid-Manhattan Library; the Greenwich Library; the Perrot Library, Old Greenwich, Connecticut, and the indispensable Interlibrary Loan Service have supplied me with most of the books in the bibliography, and I thank all of those staffs.

Helene Kolosovich read the manuscript and made helpful suggestions for clarifications and nuances.

For illustrations, I am particularly indebted to Ellen Scaruffi, curator of the Bakhmeteff Archive in the Rare Books Library of Columbia University, and her staff for the time they took to guide me through their treasure house of pictures from Imperial Russia. Roy Kaufman of the Council for American Soviet Friendship, Cleveland, and the Picture Collection of the Mid-Manhattan Library also provided much material. For specific pictures, I am grateful to John Auba of the German Information Service, Gabor Menczel of the Hungarian consulate, and Sovfoto, all in New York; to Mary Finch of the Office of Presidential Libraries in the National Archives, Washington, D.C., and Barbara Henckel at the White House; and to the Amsterdam Historic Museum and to Carl Nix, curator of the Atlas van Stolk Collection, Rotterdam. My editor at Atheneum has provided wise and patient counsel throughout the creation of this our third book together.

Most of all I am indebted to my wife and undaunted traveling companion, Charlene, for her help throughout the years of this writing project. Her sharp eyes and keen ears more than doubled the knowledge I gained while in the four republics, and while the momentous developments of the past year unfolded.

May 1992
Old Greenwich, Connecticut

CONTENTS

GERMANY

Baltic Sea

Gulf of Finland

FINLAND

CZECHOSLOVAKIA

HUNGARY

POLAND

Estonia

Lake Ladoga

Latvia

Narva

Lithuania

Brest

• Minsk

Saint Petersburg
Leningrad
Petrograd

Arkhangel'sk

Byelorussia

U

Chernobyl

• R.

ROMANIA

Kiev •

Moscow •

Gorky •

Russia

URAL MOUNTAINS

S

Moldavia

Ukraine

Poltava

Dnieper R.

Don R.

• Tobolsk

Sevastopol

CRIMEA

Volga R.

Sterlitamak •

• Sverdlovsk

Yalta

Kerch

• Azov

U n i o n

Stalingrad
Volgograd

Sea of Azov

TURKEY

Black Sea

Stavropol

o f

Georgia

CAUCASUS

Gori •

Caspian Sea

Rubtsov

Tbilisi

Armenia

MTNS.

Kazakhstan

Azerbaijan

Uzbekistan

Turkmenistan

Tashkent •

IRAN

Samarkand

Kirgizia

Tadzhikistan

AFGHANISTAN

HIMALAYA MOUNTAINS

PAKISTAN

INDIA

Map by Virginia Norey

The USSR in 1989

Peter the Great at age twenty-five,
on his first visit to western Europe
Library of Congress

CHAPTER ONE
PETER
THE GIANT

D EATH TO THE TRAITORS! DEATH TO THE TRAITORS!"
Young Peter heard the shout repeated over and over, coming through the palace windows from the open square of the Kremlin. It was the guards shouting, the special *streltsy* regiments responsible for protecting the city of Moscow. But what were they doing inside the walls of the Kremlin, the ancient fortress home of the rulers of Russia? And what traitors were they shouting about? The czar, Peter's half brother, had died a few days before, on April 27, 1682, and there was a problem naming a new czar because he had no children. But the nobles and men of the church had met as they always did when a czar died. Some wanted to name Peter's other half brother, Ivan, and some wanted to name Peter himself. When they asked the crowd in the Kremlin Square that day, the crowd had roared, "Peter!" So it seemed settled. Peter would be crowned the new czar. And since he was only ten years old, his mother would be named regent, to help him rule. And wise old Artamon Matveyev, who had been his mother's guardian when she was young, would advise them both. The problem was solved. What traitors were the guards shouting about?

Listening closely, Peter heard another shout that answered his question in a frightening way. "Kill the Naryshkins!" the guards shouted.

1

Peter's mother was a member of the Naryshkin family. She would explain to him what was going on.

While the guards kept shouting, Peter's mother and Artamon Matveyev called Peter to come to them. They called Ivan too. Not much use explaining anything to Ivan. Though he was six years older than Peter, he seemed almost dim-witted—at least, he usually said so little it was hard to tell if he was thinking anything at all. It seemed strange that he and Ivan were sons of the same man. Their father was Czar Alexis, who was the son of the first czar chosen from the Romanov family, Czar Mikhail. But of course there was a major difference. Ivan was the child of Czar Alexis's first wife, and Peter was the child of his second wife.

Peter's mother explained to the two boys that the guards had stormed into the Kremlin because they had heard a rumor that she had murdered Ivan to make sure her son Peter was the next czar. The rumor was apparently started by Ivan's sister, Sophia, now twenty-five years old. Sophia wanted Ivan to be named czar.

Artamon Matveyev said the way to prove that the rumor was false was for Peter's mother to show the yelling mob that both boys were very much alive. Frightening as it was, she must take them onto the palace porch overlooking the square. The brave young woman gave one hand to Peter and the other hand to Ivan and led them out. The crowd quieted enough to hear her say that they could see for themselves that both boys were safe. Then she took them back inside.

But truth and falsehood have little weight with an excited mob. After a few minutes some of the guards rushed inside the palace to where Peter, his mother, Ivan, and Matveyev were still standing. They seized Matveyev, carried him out onto that same porch, and threw him off. As Peter watched, the old man landed on the sharp pikes held by the guards still in the square, and died a bloody death.

One death was not enough. The guards again shouted, "Kill the Naryshkins!" They searched the palace until they found two of Peter's uncles, his mother's brothers. They carried them away, along with a number of nobles who were friends of the Naryshkin family. Some of their captives they tortured, to try to get them to confess to a plot to murder Ivan. Most of the captives they killed over the next few days.

The guards did not harm Peter and his mother physically. But the horror of that day stayed with them the rest of their lives.

There was no plot to murder Ivan. When Ivan's sister Sophia failed in her effort to discredit Peter and his mother, she next proposed that Ivan and Peter share the title of czar, and persuaded the *streltsy* regiments to support this idea. Peter's mother, having lost her wisest counselor, two of her brothers, and many of her friends, was unable to resist. Next the *streltsy* demanded that Sophia be the regent, instead of Peter's mother.

On June 6, 1682, the two boys were crowned in the Cathedral of the Assumption in Moscow as Ivan V and Peter I, co-czars of all the Russias. They sat on a specially made double throne. There was an opening in the throne's back, so that Sophia could stand behind it and whisper to them what to say as they ruled the nation.

Actually, neither of the boys needed to concern himself much with ruling. Sophia chose some good advisers and with their help cared for the nation quite well for the next seven years. Peter and his mother left the Kremlin palace and its memories and went to live in the outskirts of Moscow, where there was more air to breathe and less ceremony to tie down a growing boy. Leaving the Kremlin, Peter also left his teachers and his lessons. After that, his education had no formal plan. But he had an enormous curiosity, and he learned a great deal about subjects that interested him by asking endless questions of people he met.

A favorite subject for Peter, as for many boys, was war. At one of the palaces where he lived, he organized all the boys, whether they were from noble families or sons of stable hands, into regiments and drilled them constantly. Following a principle that he kept all his life, he awarded promotion to a higher rank entirely on the basis of merit, without regard to wealth or birth. Peter himself advanced slowly from rank to rank. In time, when all the boys were grown up, Peter would make that regiment the first unit of a new Russian Imperial Guard.

Another interest developed almost by accident. One day in June 1688, when Peter was sixteen, he was poking around in a shed on the palace grounds. He found an old boat, twenty feet long and six feet wide, and different in design from any boat he had seen on the rivers of Russia. He inquired about it. It was an English sailboat, he learned, though its mast and sails had long since disappeared. It had been a wonderful boat, one that could take a man where he wanted to go, even sailing against the wind. That idea appealed to Peter greatly. He asked to have this English boat restored, its mast and sails replaced.

In a few weeks the boat was launched on a nearby river, and Peter quickly learned how to sail it. This new sport delighted him, and like all amateur sailors, he soon wanted a larger boat and a larger body of water to sail on. That summer he took some workmen to a lake eighty-five miles from Moscow, where they began to build boats. Peter, who all his life loved working with wood, joined energetically in the building. When he had to return to the capital in September, he directed that the work be continued through the winter so that the boats would be ready by spring.

In the meantime, Peter had to fulfill a responsibility as a member of the Romanov family. At sixteen, he was considered old enough to marry and become a father, in order that the family might continue to rule Russia for many generations. He was not allowed, however, to find for himself the girl he would marry. Royal weddings in all countries were arranged. Peter's mother found the bride. She chose a shy, devout daughter of a noble Russian family, Eudoxia Loupkhina. The bride was more than three years older than the groom. Peter was a teenager, big for his age, bursting with energy, who found it almost impossible to stay in one place for more than a few minutes. Eudoxia was all of twenty, and much more sedate. Peter agreed to his mother's selection without a lot of enthusiasm, and the wedding took place in January 1689.

Close acquaintance with his wife did not increase Peter's enthusiasm. Eudoxia was not interested in any of the hundreds of new ideas he was always exploring. Peter loved to talk with the many foreigners who lived in Moscow about their native countries. Russian ways were all Eudoxia cared about, and she was actually afraid of the foreigners.

When spring came, the bridegroom set out for the lake to see his new boats. He would have spent the whole summer sailing, but in August his mother sent him word it was vital he return to Moscow.

For seven years Sophia had looked after the government, with the help of numerous relatives. But Peter's mother and her family were not satisfied to have Sophia ruling. They formed a plan to overthrow her. Copying Sophia's methods, they spread their own rumor, that Sophia and the *streltsy* were plotting to attack Peter. In the middle of the night Peter went to a monastery about fifty miles from Moscow. His mother and his wife, now pregnant, joined him there. Peter summoned troops loyal to him to come to the monastery. Others came without being called. Then Peter denounced several of Sophia's ministers, saying they were involved in the plot to kill him. He proposed to his co-czar, Ivan, that they rule without Sophia. Enough nobles and troops supported

Peter in this proposal to force Ivan to agree. Peter sent Sophia to live in a convent near Moscow, to be visited only by her aunts and sisters. Since Ivan, now twenty-three, was still unable to play any part in government, Peter's mother and her relatives became the new rulers of Russia.

In March 1690 Eudoxia gave birth to a son, whom Peter named Alexis, after his father. The Romanov family's succession to the throne seemed assured. Peter was free to go back to doing whatever most interested him. It was six more years before he really concerned himself with governing.

Much of the six years Peter spent in a section of Moscow called the "German suburb." That was home to dozens of merchants and craftsmen, soldiers and sailors, from Germany and also from Holland, England, and Scotland. They had come to Russia over a period of decades to make their fortunes, and many had liked life there well enough to stay. They built houses similar to those they had left in western Europe, dressed in European clothes, and ate European food. Young Peter found a lot more fun in the German suburb than in the stuffy halls of his palaces. And the Europeans enjoyed answering the endless questions of this ruler who wore his crown so lightly.

Peter was not the only Russian who loved fun, of course. Before long he was leading a group of more than a hundred men of all ages and ranks in pursuit of pleasure. Peter named this group the Jolly Company and had a huge mansion constructed for its use. The only qualification for membership was that the czar find a man's company enjoyable. Some of his favorite Europeans were included, with a Swiss, Francis Lefort, becoming in time Peter's closest friend.

In the summer of 1693 Peter decided to see for himself the great merchant ships the Europeans talked about. Russia's only port was Arkhangel'sk, near the Arctic Circle, a thousand miles north of Moscow. Peter traveled there, took a short voyage on one of the ships, and so became the first czar to sail on salt water. More important, he talked with many ships' captains, especially those of Holland, one of the leading seafaring nations of that time. He grew fascinated with that small country, grown rich through trade on all the oceans of the world.

When Peter was twenty-one, his mother died. Two years later, in February 1696, his co-czar, Ivan, died. Peter was now the supreme ruler of Russia, at age twenty-three. His half brother Ivan had been notable for his weakness. Peter was notable for his strength of both body and mind. He was six feet seven inches tall, a giant in a time when the average height of men was less than it is today. He had long arms and powerful hands, callused by the carpenter's work he loved. Unlike the Russian nobility, he wore no beard, only a small mustache in the European fashion. But he rejected the European custom of wearing a wig; he had his auburn brown hair cut to halfway between his ears and his shoulders. His intelligence and originality of thought were remarkable, and the curiosity and desire for new knowledge he displayed as a boy stayed with him all his life.

Two other characteristics of the ruler also developed early. He had very little patience and a very hot temper. Both his servants and his friends suffered from his anger, often unjustly. Usually he quickly forgave and forgot. But one episode remained in his memory forever: the storming of the Kremlin by the *streltsy* when he was ten years old. He knew that the ruler of Russia must always be on guard against plots to overthrow him.

Some biographers believe the horror of that scene marked more than Peter's memory. Strong as he was, he suffered from one physical malady. Sometimes in moments of stress the muscles on the left side of his face would begin to twitch. Occasionally the twitching spread to his left arm, which moved without his being able to control it, suggesting to some a mild form of epileptic convulsion. A cause more probable than the horror Peter had seen was a high fever he once suffered. This may have damaged a small portion of his brain that controlled movements on his left side. Whatever the cause, the attacks caused Peter acute embarrassment. But they usually passed quickly, especially if there was a close friend present to ease his stress.

The country Peter ruled was the largest in the world, then as now. In the northwest it bordered Finland, in Peter's day part of the empire of Sweden. In the west it bordered Poland. In the southwest it bordered the lands of the Turks and Tatars that encircled the Black Sea and Caspian Sea. In the southeast it bordered China, ruled by the Manchu dynasty. In the east it touched the Pacific Ocean. And in the north it stretched well above the Arctic Circle, to a seacoast blocked by ice for half the year. The distance west to east was six thousand miles. In all this vast land there were only eight million people. Most of them lived in the western third of the nation. East of the Ural Mountains was Siberia, a wilderness barely explored and largely uninhabited.

Russia was rich in minerals, in farmland, and in forests. But she had developed her natural wealth much less than had the nations of western Europe. Peter knew that from his conversations in the German suburb and in Arkhangel'sk. His first order of business was to increase contacts and trade with the rest of the world. Russia's only port, Arkhangel'sk, was accessible only when the Arctic ice melted. The Baltic Sea was not far from Russia's western border, but all shipping on the Baltic was controlled by Sweden. The Black Sea was not far from her southern border, but all shipping on that sea was controlled by the Turks.

If Peter could break the Turkish blockade, Russian ships could sail down the mighty Don River, 1,325 miles long, across the Black Sea to the Mediterranean and the whole world. The first step was to capture a Turkish fort controlling the mouth of the Don, at the town of Azov. Peter's first attempt, a land attack, failed.

He developed a better plan. He built on the banks of the Don a fleet of twenty-five war galleys, powered like those of the ancient Romans both by sail and by many long oars. Then he took personal command of an amphibious attack force, consisting of land troops, artillery, 1,300 river barges, and those swift galleys.

Peter's sister, Natalya, fearing for his safety, wrote to him begging him not to "go near the enemy's cannonballs and bullets." Peter, elated by real warfare, wrote back, "It is not I who go near to cannonballs and bullets, but they come near to me. Send orders for them to stop it."

Azov fell in two months and Peter returned to Moscow for his first victory parade. Again he followed a Roman model: A procession of soldiers and horses several miles long passed through a triumphal arch erected for the occasion. Peter's high-ranking commanders rode in gilded carriages. But Peter himself walked the nine-mile route across the city with the captains of the galleys that had insured the victory.

As would be expected, Peter ordered his shipyard on the Don to build larger ships, large enough to sail on the open sea. He would give his country a navy to defeat the Turkish fleet. Because Russia lacked ports, the Russians had no tradition as seafarers. Peter met this problem in two ways. He instructed his ambassadors all over Europe to recruit men who knew the sea to come to Russia to build ships and command naval forces. And he determined that Russians should learn not only the arts of the sea but other useful modern knowledge as well.

To this end he organized a group of 250 Russians, led by three ambassadors, to go to western Europe. If possible the ambassadors were also to gain support for a war against the Turks. Peter called the group the Great Embassy and directed it to visit the countries with the most ships and the best sailors: Holland and England. Also on the itinerary were short visits to other nations along the way. Purposely omitted was a visit to the most powerful nation in Europe, France under King Louis XIV, for France was known to be friendly to the Turks.

When the Great Embassy left Moscow on March 20, 1697, one of its members was a tall young man dressed in ordinary clothes, who called himself Peter Mikhailov and said he was going on the journey to learn carpentry. Peter was not about to miss this great adventure. But he knew if he traveled as czar of all the Russias he would have to spend too much time at boring dinners given for him by the rulers of the countries he visited and would not be able to learn by working side by side with shipwrights and other practical, useful men. He commanded that no one reveal his true identity. Still, it was impossible to disguise a height of six feet seven inches.

No czar had ever left Russia before. There was great curiosity about Peter in all the countries he passed through. Crowds formed on the streets to see him go by. But when his fellow rulers saw he sincerely wanted to avoid royal pomp, they made arrangements for him to meet the people who were doing the work that interested him.

In Holland he worked for four months as a carpenter in a shipyard and earned a certificate stating that Peter Mikhailov was "an able and competent shipwright." When the ship he had helped build was launched, the master of the shipyard gave it to Peter as a gift from the city of Amsterdam. A Dutch admiral assembled hundreds of ships to stage a mock battle in his honor. Peter, delighted, insisted on being in the middle of the action.

The microscope had been invented in Holland a few years before. Peter visited the inventor and looked at the "tiny animals" the microscope made visible. He visited a hospital and tried his hand at pulling teeth and at dissecting a corpse. He admired the wonderful ice skates that carried the Dutch quickly along their frozen canals. And, his masterful biographer Robert Massie wryly states, he might have met the great painter Rembrandt, but the paintings Peter wanted to take home were pictures of ships.

After five months in Holland the Great Embassy moved on to England. There Peter was treated to another mock sea battle by King William III. He visited the houses of Parliament, where he insisted on staying outside and looking at proceedings through a window instead of being formally received. He liked what he saw and commented, "It is good to hear subjects speaking truthfully and openly to their king. This is what we must learn from England." He visited the royal arsenal, and the royal mint, which was directed by Sir Isaac Newton, though the great scientist was away from London at Cambridge University at the time of Peter's visit. The English Quaker leader William Penn came to call on Peter, and found they could talk to each other in Dutch; Peter had picked up some of that language. Peter attended several Quaker meetings for worship, both before and after Penn's visit. He also received a visit from a dignitary of the Church of England, the bishop of Salisbury. (Peter had no thought of forsaking the Russian Orthodox faith, but he had many ideas on how its practices might be improved.)

THE GREAT EMBASSY RECRUITED SIXTY ENGLISHMEN TO GO TO work in Russia. Most were connected with ships in one way or another, but two were barbers. Peter found the fashions of Europe much more practical than the cumbersome robes and long beards of the Russian nobility. He had decided, back in the German suburb, not to wear a beard. Now he had in mind a lot more work for those barbers in Russia.

In May 1698, fourteen months after they had set out from Moscow, the Russians left England and headed home. On the way they visited Austria. Their primary purpose there was diplomatic negotiations in Vienna with Leopold I, emperor of the Holy Roman Empire. Only fifteen years earlier a Turkish invasion had almost reached Vienna before Leo-

---

OVERLEAF:

Peter loved ships. During his stay in Holland in 1697
the Dutch staged this mock sea battle for his pleasure.
Amsterdam Historic Museum; painted by Abraham Storck

pold's armies drove it back. Now Leopold had at last won a decisive victory over the Turks and was about to sign a peace treaty. Peter hoped Leopold would help him open the Black Sea to ships of all nations. But Leopold wanted no more trouble in the east, so that all his armies would be free to thwart the ambitions of Louis XIV of France in the west.

On July 15, 1698, as Peter was preparing to leave Vienna to visit Venice and Rome, he received news that those troublesome *streltsy* regiments were spreading rumors that the czar had died on his long trip. They were trying to seize power. Peter canceled the rest of the Great Embassy.

In a few days more news arrived. The guards' revolt was suppressed. It was still worrying, though. Was there a deeper plot against Peter? He must find out. But there was time for one more diplomatic visit. The route home lay across Poland, which was ruled by a young man only two years older than Peter. His name was Augustus. Peter stopped to get acquainted, and after four days the two men were good friends. Poland was also without a seaport because Sweden had seized all her coast on the Baltic. Peter and Augustus discussed the possibility of joining forces to recapture the Baltic ports that had once belonged to their respective nations. Then Peter returned to Moscow, arriving September 4, 1698. He had been away a year and a half.

It was good to be back. The trip had changed Peter, had changed Europe's view of Russia, and was soon to change Russia in many ways. Peter turned his attention immediately to the revolt of the *streltsy*. Four regiments had taken part. They had said that Peter had died on his journey, that Peter's son, Alexis, then eight years old, should be named czar, and that Sophia should be made regent again. Regiments loyal to Peter had easily overcome the rebels and made them prisoners. Peter ordered that all these prisoners be questioned as to who had led the revolt, but even the cruel torture that regularly accompanied questioning in the seventeenth century got no information. To show that he would tolerate no opposition to his rule, Peter had most of the rebels over twenty years old executed. Those under twenty he exiled from Moscow after having them marked with a red-hot brand. There was no evidence that Sophia had suggested the revolt, but to insure that she would not serve as a rallying point for any rebellion in the future, Peter made her confinement in the convent permanent.

Peter's wife, Eudoxia, still had no interest in modern European ideas, which meant she was even less attractive to Peter after his trip than before. Divorce was not possible in the Russian Orthodox religion. But Peter found a way to escape his youthful marriage. If Eudoxia were to take vows as a nun, all her previous vows would be canceled. Peter simply ordered her to do this and sent her off to live a holy life. Peter's sister, Natalya, was given responsibility for raising the heir to the throne, Alexis. Peter, always involved in some new project, saw little of his son in the years that followed.

In the months after Peter's return he introduced many changes in Russia. His first day back, with his own hands he cut off the long beards of every noble he saw. He decreed that every Russian man except peasants and members of the clergy must be clean-shaven. The two barbers he had brought from England could train Russian barbers.

A year later he decreed that the long robes Russians wore must be shortened to a more practical length. A year after that he ordered the upper classes to wear French or German fashions. The guards at the gates of Moscow were given orders to cut off at the knees the long coats of visitors ignoring this decree. And he introduced a new way of rewarding a man for exceptional service to the czar. Instead of giving him a piece of land he gave him a medal.

Obviously none of these changes were very popular with the upper classes in a country whose people had always been resistant to change. But Peter knew change was necessary if his country was to be strong. It was the largest country in the world, yet invaders had repeatedly defeated Russian armies and captured border territories. The Turkish fleet still controlled the Black Sea. Peter was determined Russia should have a port open to trade all year long.

In 1700 Peter put into action the plan he had discussed with Augustus of Poland to win back from Sweden their former territories along the Baltic coast. The king of Sweden, Charles XII, was only eighteen, even younger than Peter and Augustus. But Charles's father had left him an excellent army, and the young Swede thought of little except the glory of battle. He developed into a brilliant commander and was Peter's major foe for a decade.

In the summer of 1700 Peter's regiments laid siege to the strongly fortified port city of Narva in what is now Estonia. When the city had

Young King Charles XII of Sweden led his troops to victory
over the Russians in the Battle of Narva in 1700.
New York Public Library Picture Collection

not fallen by the beginning of winter, Peter left the siege lines to confer with Augustus. While he was away, Charles transported an army of his highly trained Swedish troops to Narva, routed a much larger number of Russians, and broke the siege.

For two years after that defeat Peter worked at training his men and providing them with more modern weapons. Then in 1702 he attacked in a new location. The Neva River flows from Russia west into the Baltic. Peter personally led a successful attack on a Swedish fort on the Neva. The next spring his forces occupied the whole north shore of the Neva and defeated a Swedish fleet on the river. Russia had access to the sea at last. Peter meant to keep it.

The next step was to build a Russian fortress to command the mouth of the Neva River. For a site, Peter chose an island. He put his soldiers to work carrying earth and timber for the fortress walls and building a three-room log house where he could live and supervise construction. He also commanded that a cathedral be built inside the fort.

After the fort came port facilities for trade. Peter ordered a shipyard built on the south shore opposite the fortress, and next to the shipyard, offices for his growing navy. Construction was difficult because the location was largely marshland, with no nearby sources of stone or wood. But Peter planned a network of canals, similar to the ones he had seen in Amsterdam, to drain the marshes. He ordered materials to be brought by land and by sea, and conscripted thousands of men from all over Russia to do the work.

The next step followed naturally—the construction of a city. Peter named it Saint Petersburg, after his patron saint. The city became his chief delight in life, near the sea he loved, and a symbol of the realization of his goal of Russian access to that sea. In his mind Moscow, with its gloomy palaces and even gloomier memories, could not compare with his vision of Saint Petersburg. He brought architects from Italy and France to make his vision a reality. In 1712 he would move the government to the new city. For now he insisted that his royal relatives and members of the nobility join him in living there.

Furthermore, Peter commanded the nobles not only to live in Saint Petersburg, but to build handsome houses there. This was very expensive because of the construction problems of the location. Food was also expensive, since it had to be brought from a distance. Of course there was a lot of grumbling among the noble families, but Peter was the czar.

The conscripted workers suffered much more than the nobles did. The worst hardship of all was the climate. Saint Petersburg is located farthest north of all the major cities of the world. Many workers died

The first building of the new city Saint Petersburg was a fortress,
followed soon after by a cathedral with a dome and spire.
Library of Congress

in the marshes from the cold and from disease. There was a grim saying
that Saint Petersburg was a "city built on bones."

Later generations of Russians tended to balance the darkness of those
deaths against a glowing pride in Peter's creation. Rulers after him added
more canals, palaces, and gardens, which made the city so beautiful it
is called "the Venice of the North." Today it is the most popular destination for visitors to Peter's country.

Peter's city would be Russia's "window to Europe," as he put it. And
he had another reason to be glad at this time. He had found a woman
to love and to share his pleasure in his accomplishments. She was not
at all a woman his mother would have chosen for him, but she suited
Peter much better than the wellborn, well-educated, pious Eudoxia. She
was none of those things, but she was attractive, vigorous enough to
keep up with Peter's giant energy, and wise enough to understand him

as a man. Martha Skavronskaya was born on a farm in Estonia. One of Peter's best friends noticed her there in 1703 and brought her to Moscow, where she took the more Russian name Catherine. Peter married her secretly in 1707 and married her again in a public ceremony in 1712. She often accompanied him on his constant travels. When she did not, the two sent each other frequent tender letters and gifts of favorite foods—oysters for Catherine when possible. The most effective treatment for the facial twitch that plagued Peter was for his beloved Catherine to take his head in her hands. She bore Peter twelve children. One of their daughters would one day rule Russia.

PETER DID MUCH MORE TO CHANGE THE GOVERNMENT OF RUSSIA than change its location from Moscow. He had little respect for the council of nobles that had traditionally advised the czar. In its place he appointed a nine-member senate, which he said was responsible for governing the country when he was away from the capital. Actually Peter governed the country wherever he was, and the senate merely carried out his ideas. He set up new government offices to collect taxes, regulate trade, supervise the armed forces, and administer the laws. These offices were similar to the cabinet departments of the United States government, and to the ministries Peter had seen in western Europe. They were staffed by men chosen for their ability instead of for their connections to noble families.

One other office was responsible for protecting the czar from any efforts to overthrow his government. It used a network of secret police and informers. This office had existed in Russia for a long time, and it seemed to Peter absolutely necessary to continue it; he still remembered the day when the *streltsy* had shed so much of his family's blood.

In order to make Russia strong and prosperous Peter introduced many ideas he had acquired on the Great Embassy. In Russia only the upper classes and some of the churchmen could read and write. He ordered the establishment of public schools. Peter himself kept to the Russian Orthodox faith but decreed that Russia, like Holland, should have freedom of religion. He sent expeditions to explore the coast of Siberia, to see if the great natural resources of that region could be brought out by ship instead of by the long journey overland. He encouraged trade with his neighbors to the east, China and Japan.

Charles XII of Sweden was not at all pleased by the thought of a strong and prosperous Russia. After Charles lost the land along the banks of the Neva River to Peter, he boasted that he would capture the czar's new port once it was finished. In the meantime he intended to take Peter's ally King Augustus of Poland out of the contest for control of the Baltic Sea. This took Charles longer than he expected, but by 1708 Swedish armies controlled Poland. Almost immediately Charles crossed the Russian border and began an advance toward Moscow.

Charles found that the czar's troops were much better trained now, but they still could not stop the Swedes. Then Charles met the two age-old defenses of Russia: great distances and bitter winter. All armies of that time counted on "living off the land," taking food from the country they were passing through. But Peter ordered his soldiers to burn all the crops in the Russian fields that lay in the path of the Swedish advance. And he attacked the Swedish wagons bringing in supplies. Charles, deep inside Russian territory but still five hundred miles from Moscow, made camp for the winter just east of the city of Kiev. The winter of 1708–1709 was one of record cold, and the Swedish troops suffered terribly.

When spring came Charles began a siege of the town of Poltava. Finally in June 1709 Peter decided the time was right for a major battle. Peter and his army went to Poltava.

On his twenty-seventh birthday Charles was overseeing preparations for battle. He was always heedless of enemy bullets, riding along the front line in plain view. That day a lucky Russian musket shot wounded him in the foot, making it impossible for him to ride a horse. When the battle began eleven days later, on June 28, he had to leave close supervision of the regiments to his generals. Without Charles's overall direction the generals failed to coordinate their movements, and Peter defeated the Swedes decisively. Charles's officers persuaded their king to avoid capture by escaping south across the border into Turkey. Most of his army surrendered to Peter.

The Battle of Poltava is regarded as one of the turning points in world history. For the first time a Russian czar had defeated a powerful western monarch. Now Russia would have to be considered a major player in the international game of strategy, an ally to be sought. Peter had succeeded in making his country a part of Europe.

To promote good relations with his neighbors Peter used the customary method of arranging marriages. His niece Anne, daughter of co-

The armies of Peter and Charles XII met again in 1709,
at Poltava in Ukraine, and this time Peter was the victor.
New York Public Library Picture Collection

czar Ivan, married a German duke, and Peter's son Alexis married a German princess.

Peter expected Alexis to succeed him as czar someday. Instead, this eldest son became a great sorrow. Peter, always active, often traveling, saw little of the boy, but he tried to provide him with an education that would prepare him to rule. Alexis had little interest in ruling, having inherited from his mother, Eudoxia, a love of a quiet life devoted to learning and religion. When Alexis reached age twenty-five Peter, in desperation, sent him an ultimatum:

> My heart is . . . penetrated with grief . . . seeing that you, my son, reject all means of making yourself capable of governing well after me. . . . You even

19

will not so much as hear warlike exercises mentioned. . . . I do not exhort you to make war without lawful reasons; I only desire you to apply yourself to learn the art of it. For it is impossible to govern well without knowing the rules and disciplines of it, be it for no other end than for the defense of the country.

He threatened to name another heir unless Alexis accepted responsibility for carrying on his father's work.

Of course this was not a private problem of a father and son. There were still powerful families in Moscow who opposed all the changes Peter had made. They saw that Alexis would be just the kind of czar they wanted, one who would allow them to undo most of what Peter had done. They gave Alexis some bad advice: He could avoid his father's pressure by leaving Russia for a time. That is what the young man did, traveling secretly to Vienna.

Years earlier, at age eight, Alexis had obviously not instigated the brief revolt of the *streltsy* that had cut short Peter's Great Embassy to western Europe. But one objective of that revolt was to make young Alexis czar and Peter's half sister, Sophia, regent again. Peter feared Alexis's departure from Russia meant there was another revolt brewing. It was necessary to find out. That required a thorough investigation, with Alexis as the chief witness. Peter sent his most persuasive diplomat to bring Alexis back, promising him the quiet life he wanted, on condition he reveal all he had done and the names of all the people involved in his leaving Russia. Alexis returned to Moscow. But his answers in the investigation were evasive, leaving the suspicion he had taken part in treason against the czar. Peter, tormented by what was happening to his son, prayed for eight days for God to "instruct him what the honor and welfare of the nation required."

Some historians have called Peter a cruel tyrant who killed his own son. The facts are much more complex than that. In Russia a person accused of treason was questioned under torture to try to get all possible information about a plot. Peter did not intervene in his son's case. After two sessions with the harsh Russian whip called the knout, Alexis was willing to confess anything. A court sentenced him to die. Peter could not bring himself to sign the sentence. Two days later word came from the prison that Alexis was dying and wanted to see his father. Peter went to him, forgave him, and blessed him. Alexis died, officially of apoplexy, but more likely from the torture of a body never robust.

Peter himself lived for another seven years, until 1725. In those years he brought to a successful conclusion many of the projects he had undertaken for the country in the areas of foreign relations, economic development, and government structure.

Charles XII of Sweden never gave up his ambition to defeat Peter and recapture the Baltic ports. But he had other enemies to deal with first. In 1718 he was in the trenches in southern Norway, careless as always of his own safety. A Norwegian musket ball pierced his skull, killing him instantly. The Swedes, exhausted by Charles's constant wars, made peace. The peace treaty signed in 1721 ceded to Russia forever the territory necessary for the protection of Saint Petersburg. At a great celebration the Russian senate and church leaders gave Peter a new title: Peter the Great, Emperor and Father of the Fatherland.

Once peace was achieved with his northern neighbors Peter turned his attention to the south and east. He wanted to increase trade with India. To that end he forced the shah of Persia to cede to Russia the provinces on the western shore of the Caspian Sea, including part of Azerbaijan. He again attempted to increase trade with China by diplomatic means, but the Chinese emperor replied that his country had no need for Russian goods.

Peter commissioned a Danish captain in his fleet, Vitus Bering, to explore the eastern coast of Siberia to see if it was connected to the continent of North America. Bering found only fifty-three miles of water separating Siberia from Alaska—fifty-three miles of water we now call the Bering Strait. In the next century Russian fur traders would establish colonies in Alaska and California.

To increase trade inside his vast country Peter ordered the construction of canals to link together the great rivers. He continued to encourage the development of new industries. He established an Academy of Science to complete the education of the graduates of the schools he had founded earlier. He began Russia's first newspaper and encouraged the printing of books written in western Europe.

The governmental reforms Peter had begun required some adjustments based on experience. There were not enough Russians familiar with European governments to staff the ministries Peter had set up, so he had to recruit foreigners. Russian officials traditionally had not been paid by the state and often received bribes from the people they governed. Peter paid his officials and forbade them to accept bribes, but he was not able to stop the bribes completely.

In 1724 Peter was fifty-two years old. His supply of energy, once boundless, was being drained by a series of illnesses his doctors could help but not cure. He had decreed that each Russian ruler must name who would rule after him, instead of leaving the choice to the council of nobles and churchmen as was done before. Now Peter himself must name a strong person to carry on his work. His only male heir was his nine-year-old grandson, the son of Alexis. His second wife, Catherine, had given birth to six sons, but all had died in childhood. Peter and Catherine had three surviving daughters, the oldest sixteen. Peter decided to name Catherine his successor and held a ceremony to crown her empress.

That November of 1724 Peter was traveling by boat to inspect an ironworks on the Gulf of Finland. He saw another boat carrying twenty soldiers run aground. A strong wind threatened to capsize the boat and throw the soldiers into the icy gulf. Peter jumped into water up to his waist and directed their rescue. It delighted him that he had saved Russian lives by his quick action. But the chill he received aggravated his sickness, and on January 28, 1725, he died.

CHAPTER TWO
CATHERINE STEALS A CROWN

ETER THE GREAT DURING HIS REIGN INTRODUCED MANY
modern ideas into Russia. He also established a new structure of government that would enable those ideas to flourish. But the force driving the ancient country to change and modernize was Peter himself. Other forces resisted change. When Peter died in 1725 these forces threatened to undo what he had done. The three major groups opposing change were the nobles, the churchmen, and the serfs.

The highest rank of nobles in Russia were called boyars. They were given their rank by the czar, in recognition for some service they had performed. Along with a title, the czar gave the boyar ownership of a great tract of land. And that rank and land were passed along from generation to generation in a family. The most powerful of the boyars met from time to time as a council, called the Duma, to advise the czar about such matters as new laws or declarations of war. (The czars did not always take the advice of the Duma, however.) Most importantly, the boyars assembled at the death of a czar to have a share in choosing a successor.

Peter had greatly reduced the influence of the boyars in the government. He insisted that every man be judged on his merit, and that promotions in the military and the government be based only on merit.

That meant that the boyars' noble ancestry counted for very little. Many of Peter's closest friends and most trusted advisers had been born serfs. Furthermore, Peter had taken away the boyars' most valued right by issuing a decree that the czar should name his own successor. He had chosen his second wife, Catherine, to rule after him. Naturally the boyars resented the loss of their power.

The boyars also saw in Peter's modern ideas a threat to their wealth. In the past, when the czar gave a boyar land, he gave him also the right to a part of the labor of the people who lived on the land, the serfs. The serfs were not quite slaves, but they were not free either. A portion of everything they grew or made belonged to the boyar. That made the boyars very rich and kept the serfs very poor. In Peter's day, 95 percent of the population of Russia were serfs, living on land belonging either to some boyar or to the church or to the czar himself. In western Europe the institution of serfdom was being abolished. One of the great ideas of the Renaissance was that every individual had rights. But the ideas of the Renaissance had not spread to Russia. Many a European visitor commented that Russia before Peter was a country still living in the Middle Ages. That suited the boyars fine.

Peter never did propose abolition of serfdom. He himself had too much need of the serfs to build Saint Petersburg, construct his fleet, and fight in his army. But fear of such a proposal strengthened the boyars' opposition to the introduction of Western ideas.

The second group of men opposing modernization were the leaders of the church. The Orthodox church had been established as the official religion in the year 988 by Prince Vladimir of Kiev. Vladimir and his successors gave large gifts to the church and to its monasteries and convents. The boyars also gave gifts. Sometimes the gifts were tracts of land with serfs living on them. By Peter's day, one monastery near Moscow owned the land farmed by twenty thousand families. And there were more than five hundred monasteries and convents in Russia. Every village had its church and its priest. Every major city had its cathedral and many smaller churches.

Naturally the man at the head of this vast religious establishment, called the patriarch, was a man of great power. He was, in fact, the second most powerful man in the nation. Although the boyars had taken part in choosing the czar, it was the patriarch who placed the crown on his head, symbolizing the church's approval of the choice.

The monasteries of the Russian Orthodox church controlled vast lands and
thousands of serfs. This is the Trinity Monastery in Zagorsk.
Library of Congress

Peter was not an enemy of religion. His first tutor was a Russian
Orthodox monk, who not only taught the boy how to read and write
but also had him memorize quantities of Scripture and hymns. Peter
never forgot this early teaching. He would quote Scripture in the letters
he wrote. On his travels he attended mass and would often startle a
congregation by standing near the choir and joining lustily in the singing.
When Peter founded Saint Petersburg, the first two buildings he ordered
built were a fort and a cathedral. After every military victory he ordered
a mass of Te Deum to give thanks to God. His Russian Orthodox faith
was very genuine. But Peter recognized early in his life that the faith of
some of his European friends was also genuine, although they were
Roman Catholics or Protestants. When he visited western Europe on the
Great Embassy, he attended the worship of various churches and talked
with religious leaders.

When Peter decreed that all people living in Russia should be allowed
freedom to worship according to their own religions, the patriarch rightly
saw that as a first step toward reducing the power of the Russian Orthodox church. Some people in Europe were saying that church leaders

should advise governments but should not have authority in government—an early expression of what we today call the doctrine of the separation of church and state. Peter was listening to such ideas.

To reduce the conservative influence of the church in government, Peter used a simple strategy. When the patriarch died in 1700, Peter did not name a successor. Instead he appointed a temporary "guardian" of the office, who had modern ideas. Then in 1721 he abolished the office of patriarch and put the church under the control of a Holy Governing Synod, or council. This council was under the control of Peter.

Opposition to Peter's ideas by the boyars and the churchmen was based on the desire to protect their wealth and power. The third group in opposition, the serfs, had neither wealth nor power. For them, Peter's ideas for modernizing Russia threatened life itself.

Before Peter, a serf had almost no knowledge of the world beyond the village where he lived and the church where he worshiped. No one taught him to read and write. His priest, usually illiterate himself, taught memorized creeds and prayers. Parents taught their children farming and simple crafts. The serfs' only contact with the boyar who owned the land they farmed was through the agent who collected the boyar's portion of the crops. As for the czar, he was the man in Moscow demanding of the village another tax to pay for a new palace, or fresh recruits to fight a new war. If the demands of the boyar or the czar grew too heavy, a serf family could move to another village where demands were lighter or enforcement less efficient. A new recruit could often find a chance to desert from the army.

Peter's demands were unlike those of any czar before him. His vision for Russia required not one new palace or one new war, but a whole new capital city, a new army with new weapons, a navy, and a merchant fleet. That vision required a great increase in taxes. And it required recruiting not just soldiers but laborers as well, to build Saint Petersburg, to work in shipyards and weapons factories. Worse, from the point of view of the serfs, Peter's reorganization of the government made it much more difficult to escape from the tax collector and the recruiting officer.

The boyars and the churchmen expressed their opposition to Peter through various political intrigues in Moscow and Saint Petersburg, such as the effort to make his son Alexis czar in his place. The serfs took more direct action. Some, defying government orders forbidding travel,

*The most famous warriors in Russia were the cossacks, expert horsemen who
sometimes helped and sometimes opposed the ruler in Moscow.*
Atlas van Stolk Collection, Rotterdam; sketches by J. A. Langendijk

went all the way to Siberia, to live where distance from the capital
weakened the czar's power. Others traveled to the valley of the Don
River. There they joined communities of proud people known as cossacks. Cossack men had a reputation as fierce fighters on horseback,
and they had successfully resisted control by Moscow for generations.
Still other serfs listened to the fiery speeches of men organizing rebellions
against the czar, joined their small armies, and marched off to capture
control of various towns and cities for brief periods. Peter dealt with
these rebellions of the people as vigorously as he dealt with the revolt
of the *streltsy* and with the plot involving his son. But in the decades
following his death, the number and force of such rebellions increased.

Peter was strong enough to drive his changes forward in the face of
any opposition. The rulers who came after him had neither his vision
nor his strength. It was almost forty years before Russia had another
ruler inclined to modernization and strong willed enough to overcome
the opposition to it.

Peter's chosen successor, his wife, Catherine, crowned as Empress
Catherine I, died two years after Peter. She was succeeded by alternating

Romanov sons and daughters, five rulers in thirty-five years, up to 1762. Then Russia got another sovereign worthy of the title "Great"—a second Catherine, Catherine the Great.

In 1741 the only surviving child of Peter the Great, Elizabeth, had become empress of Russia. Elizabeth had no children and chose as her heir Peter's grandson, the child of her sister and a powerful German duke.

This boy, then thirteen years old, was named Peter, after his grandfather. He had been brought up in his father's house as a German, with a great admiration for the military successes of King Frederick II of Prussia. To prepare him to succeed her as a Russian ruler, Empress Elizabeth brought him to Moscow. He soon proved a great disappointment to her. He took little interest in learning about the country he would someday rule, maintaining that German ways were better than Russian ones. Almost the only thing that interested him was soldiers.

Nevertheless, he was a Romanov descendant, with the responsibility to marry and continue the Romanov imperial line. Elizabeth hoped a strong and capable wife would give him a strong son and also help him rule the country. Beyond that, every royal marriage offered a chance for forming an international alliance. When it became known that the empress of Russia was looking for a wife for her heir, more than one mother weighed the benefits and liabilities of such a match. Russia was now a major power in Europe, a desirable ally. The imperial court seemed to offer a life of considerable splendor. But the stories one heard of the Russians—their manners, their orgies, their cruelty, their clinging to medieval ways under the guidance of the Russian Orthodox church— if they were true, would a mother choose such a match for her daughter?

One mother who answered yes to that question was the sister of a future king of Sweden, the wife of the ruler of the tiny German state of Anhalt-Zerbst, southwest of Berlin. She had recognized the significance of young Peter's Romanov descent years before the empress Elizabeth named him her heir. And she had seen to it that her oldest daughter met him when both were still children. Later, when the daughter showed a keen mind and an interest in marrying well, she sent her portrait to the empress. When the girl was fourteen, in late 1743, the empress invited the mother to bring her for a visit to Moscow, with a suggestion that a marriage might result. Happily, the daughter was agreeable to the idea, though royal marriages rarely regarded the feelings of the bride or groom. The girl wrote later, "Of all the matches that had been proposed, this was the most brilliant." Although it was midwinter, mother and daughter accepted the invitation.

After a forty-day trip by sled they arrived in Moscow. The next day Peter celebrated his sixteenth birthday. He was pleased to see a German girl, since he missed very much the country where he had spent his early years. The young couple enjoyed each other's company. The empress Elizabeth was also pleased by what she saw, and before many days had gone by she decided she had chosen the right wife for Peter. Peter agreed.

There were two changes necessary before the wedding. The wife of the future czar must accept the Russian Orthodox religion. And she must have a Russian name. After several months of study with a monk the prospective bride decided she could meet these conditions and was duly baptized into the Orthodox faith, with the new name Ekaterina, the Russian form of Catherine. Two months after that she and Peter were married.

Catherine was not disappointed in her expectation of a life of splendor. She lived in ornate palaces, both in Moscow and in Saint Petersburg. She enjoyed festive dinners with good wine, followed by dancing or cards or masquerades. The members of the court received her warmly, and as she learned Russian she found that a number of the men were familiar with European books and enjoyed literary or philosophical discussions with a lady, especially one as attractive as this newcomer.

On the other hand, Catherine was definitely disappointed in Peter as a husband. He was young for his age. He had a huge collection of toy soldiers, and even at sixteen he loved drilling them in imitation of his Prussian hero Frederick II. Sometimes he would dress some of the younger members of the court in military uniforms and march them around the palace. He invited Catherine to join in this game, which she did to humor him, and he gave her long lectures on military matters. At night he would play with the toy soldiers in their bedroom until he was tired, then climb into their bed and fall asleep immediately, without so much as a good-night kiss.

Catherine was quite willing to carry out her duty to give birth to a child to continue the Romanov line, but Peter did not seem at all interested in fatherhood. She hoped he would learn to love her in time, and tried to please him every way she could. But years went by. Empress Elizabeth sent various advisers to the young couple to try to find out

A young German princess married a grandson of Peter the Great and became the empress her subjects called Catherine the Great.
Library of Congress

what the problem was. One possibility was that the responsibility of fathering a future czar frightened Peter. The practical Russians suggested he might be more at ease with a different female partner, with less at stake. That turned out to be true, and soon he was flirting, and more than flirting, with other women. But he grew more and more distant from his wife. The lady-in-waiting that the empress had made responsible for Catherine was desperate. She suggested, perhaps with the consent of the empress, a different male partner for Catherine. There were plenty of young men attracted to the young wife, and in her perplexity and grief she had found their company a pleasure. But she hesitated at being unfaithful to her husband.

Eventually the pressure for an heir drove Catherine, after seven years of unconsummated marriage, into the arms of a gentleman-in-waiting, Sergei Saltuikov. A son was born in September 1754. The empress

30

welcomed the baby joyfully, without asking questions. He was duly christened Paul and accepted into the Romanov line.

Peter and Catherine remained married, but naturally the distance between them increased still more. Peter took a mistress, an accepted arrangement in the Russia of his day. Catherine took a new lover, this time one of five brothers noted for military prowess. His name was Grigory Orlov.

The birth of the baby Paul had turned everyone's attention to the future of Russia. Peter looked to the day when as czar he could tie the country more closely to the Prussia of Frederick II. He realized that Catherine, though German born, had become a very patriotic Russian. Many Russians realized that too, while deploring Peter's continuing fondness for Prussia.

Two plans were made at court for Russia after the empress Elizabeth died. Peter planned to divorce Catherine and marry his mistress; and a group of nobles, including the Orlov brothers, planned to replace Peter as czar with the child Paul, and name Catherine regent. Before either plan was put into effect, in December 1761 Elizabeth died, and Peter became Czar Peter III.

The new czar immediately took several actions. He reduced taxes. He ended the requirement that all nobles serve in government or the military. He reaffirmed his grandfather's policy of freedom of religion and seized much of the property of the Russian Orthodox church for the state. Most important, he concluded an alliance with Frederick II and announced his intention to join him in a war against Denmark.

That was too much for the nobles. Peter had to be replaced at once. But instead of making Catherine regent, why not make her empress? Catherine had no doubt she could rule more capably than her husband, so she consented to this plan. On June 28, 1762, six months after Elizabeth's death, Grigory Orlov escorted Catherine to the barracks housing one of the four regiments of guards stationed in Saint Petersburg. Catherine told the guards that Peter planned to kill her and her son. She was a popular figure with the officers and men, and they all swore allegiance to her without bothering to check the truth of what she said. Peter was planning to divorce Catherine, not kill her, though he might have had some such thought if he had known his wife intended to steal his crown.

A second regiment that Catherine and Orlov visited was equally supportive. Then Catherine sought and got the endorsement of the leaders of the Russian Orthodox church, who gladly proclaimed her sovereign and her son her successor. The two remaining guard regiments in Saint Petersburg hurried to her side.

Once assured of the support of a strong military force and of the church, Catherine was ready to challenge her husband. She put on a uniform of a colonel of the guards, mounted a dappled gray horse, and rode out of Saint Petersburg at the head of a column of fourteen thousand soldiers. Her destination was the palace, west of the city, where Peter was. News of these events spread rapidly, with many nobles joining in to swear allegiance to Catherine. Peter hurried into a boat and sought protection at the fortified Kronstadt naval base in the harbor, only to be turned away because the navy was also supporting Catherine.

He was shut up in a palace outside the city, guarded by Grigory Orlov's brother Aleksey, who a few days later sent Catherine a note saying "our monster has fallen very sick." Catherine might have kept him in prison somewhere for the rest of his life. But the nobles knew that any person with a claim to the throne serves as a rallying point for rebellion. There had been many cases of that in Russian history. They saw to it that Peter's sickness quickly worsened and, without telling Catherine the details, soon reported that he had died. She had his body dressed in his beloved blue German uniform and buried.

In September 1762 Catherine went to Moscow to be crowned in the ancient way, in the Assumption Cathedral in the Kremlin. She professed her faith by reading aloud the creed of the Russian Orthodox church. Then she placed the crown on her head and took up the orb and scepter, symbols of authority. In a long mass an archbishop anointed her empress.

NOW IT WAS TIME FOR CATHERINE TO PROVE HER BELIEF THAT she could be a better ruler than the man she had helped overthrow. As with so many rulers, her first problem was money. Peter the Great had left the nation debt free. The empress Elizabeth had left it with a huge and growing national debt. Income of the government for 1762 was only three-fourths of expenditure. Catherine set about increasing that income.

Russia is a country with great natural resources, including rich farmland and many minerals. But the modernization program Peter the Great had worked at so vigorously still had a long way to go. Catherine sent experts around the country to introduce better farming methods, and invited immigrants from neighboring countries to till the rich Russian soil. She commissioned a geological survey, founded a school of mining, and encouraged the opening of new mines. She encouraged expansion of foreign trade, especially exports. Various noble families had been granted sole rights to manufacture certain products. Catherine ended these monopolies, allowing many new factories to be set up. In three short years she turned the government's deficit into a surplus and paid off 75 percent of its debt.

During the frustrating years of her marriage Catherine had used her time to read widely. The eighteenth century in western Europe was a time when many political ideas were being developed—ideas that led to the American Revolution and the French Revolution. These ideas were summed up by the term the *Enlightenment*. Catherine talked about such ideas with the more progressive members of the court and with Europeans who visited Russia. She saw how much Russia fell short of the ideal nation described by the philosophers of the Enlightenment.

Most of her people were serfs tied to land owned by nobles. Most of her people were illiterate. Even most of the priests were illiterate. The government reforms instituted by Peter the Great had faltered in the years since his death. Bribes were once again the chief source of income for government officials, who did little more than maintain some sort of order in the country and collect taxes to send to Moscow. The senate that Peter had established still existed, but its members had no broad knowledge of the nation they were responsible for. They had no accurate maps and no census figures. Catherine set about remedying all these lacks. She convened a legislative commission made up of 672 representatives elected by various groups in the population, including even the serfs living on land belonging to the state. She directed the commission to study government reform and the possibility of emancipation of all serfs in Russia.

The commission met for many years, discussed much, and accomplished little. Its chief importance was the opportunity it gave for the people to present their grievances. But in the meantime Catherine took a number of direct actions. She provided adequate salaries for provincial governors. Then she required them to provide the services customarily expected from government. She made them responsible for repairing roads and bridges. She ordered that "people's schools" be established and made available to children from the age of five—even children who were girls. Building a system of public education, of course, took time, since there were few who knew enough to teach.

Catherine established Russia's first college of medicine to train doctors to deal with the enormous health needs of her people. She set an example by submitting to the recently developed procedure of inoculation against smallpox, an example followed by nearly two hundred of the gentry, including Grigory Orlov.

The Orlov brothers were very much a part of Catherine's reign in the early years. Aleksey Orlov commanded her military forces against enemies foreign and domestic. Catherine wanted to make Grigory Orlov her husband after her coronation. He was already the father of her second son, and was recognized and accepted as her lover. But statecraft dictated that Catherine find a more royal husband—or keep open the possibility of an international alliance sealed by marriage. So Grigory continued for ten years as court favorite—a difficult role for a man of action. He became more and more restless, then ill-tempered, until Catherine finally sent him abroad on a diplomatic mission.

When Grigory returned he found Catherine had a new lover of a calmer sort, an officer twenty-eight years old. She was forty-three. Grigory was furious at first, but Catherine reasoned with him and gave him many gifts and the title of prince. Grigory in return gave Catherine a diamond of 199 carats, which she gave to the nation to adorn the royal scepter.

This end of their long affair shows how well Grigory knew Catherine. He knew how much she loved splendor. She once ordered a crown decorated with five thousand diamonds. She remodeled many palaces, enlarging them and enhancing their interiors. The most famous is the Hermitage in Saint Petersburg, which she had built to house her collection of nearly four thousand masterpieces of European painting. She replaced so many public buildings in Saint Petersburg that it was said she found it a city of wood and left it a city of granite.

But beyond splendor Grigory knew how much Catherine valued the companionship, the comfort, the counsel of a man—needs her husband, Peter, had failed so completely to supply. The twenty-eight-year-old officer would be succeeded in time by another and another favorite. One of them, another Grigory, Grigory Potemkin, has a name almost as famous as her own. The final count runs to more than twenty lovers. Such a record has suggested to some, in her own time and since, that Catherine was primarily interested in sex, and indeed she has been so depicted in some books and films. But such a view neglects the serious side of a ruler who accomplished much for her adopted country.

The reforms of government Catherine suggested to the legislative commission came slowly. She had quicker success in what we would call "power politics," aided by strong advisers and allies. In short, she made a very large country even larger.

Russia's neighbor on the west, Poland, had become weak by Catherine's day. Poland was ruled by an elected king, who served for life. A year after Catherine was crowned empress, that king died. Catherine used her influence to have elected a young Pole she knew well. Through him she had considerable control over Poland. But Poland's Prussian neighbor, Frederick II, proposed a more direct control. He suggested that Prussia, Russia, and Austria each seize a slice of Poland. They did so in 1772 and again in 1793. Then in 1795 they divided up what Polish territory was left, so that Poland ceased to exist. In that way Catherine acquired all the region of Ukraine.

The dream of Peter the Great to give Russia access to the Black Sea had still not been fulfilled. The Turks again controlled all the Black Sea coast, which included the mouths of several large Russian rivers. The Turks recognized Catherine's desire to expand south and, in hopes of discouraging her, used a small border incident in 1768 as a pretext to declare war on Russia. Catherine responded by sending an army against the Turks. She also startled the world by sending the Russian navy, under the overall command of Aleksey Orlov, completely around Europe and through the Mediterranean to fight them. In Chesme Bay on the Turkish coast Orlov destroyed twelve Turkish warships. Then Catherine's best general, Aleksandr Suvorov, advanced to within 250 miles of the Turkish capital, Constantinople, and the Turks made peace. By treaty Catherine was given the right to send merchant ships through the Black Sea, received possession of the ports of Azov and Kerch at the mouth of the Don River, and had the large peninsula known as the Crimea declared independent of Turkish control.

Catherine's successes did not mean that all Russians supported her or her policies. In her huge domain there were still rebel groups fighting for one cause or another. One such was a community of cossacks living on the lower Don River who belonged to a conservative religious sect called Old Believers. Both Peter the Great and Peter III had left them alone, but when Catherine strengthened provincial governments she threatened their independent way of life. One cossack, Yemelyan Pugachov, hit on an effective scheme to rally resistance. He proclaimed that he was actually Peter III, dethroned by his wife but still alive and the rightful ruler of Russia. He recruited an army of twenty-five thousand cossacks and serfs and led them toward Moscow. It was the most serious rebellion of Catherine's reign, and she reacted strongly and effectively.

Pugachov was defeated and executed. But he had brought about a change in Catherine. Her view of the possibilities of government based on the principles of the Enlightenment was marred. Her determination to preserve her power as monarch was strengthened. It was her duty to pass that power on intact. Her determination became even stronger in 1789 when the French Revolution began, which eventually deposed and then beheaded King Louis XVI and his queen, Marie Antoinette.

Now, instead of encouraging the spread of Western ideas in Russia, Catherine changed to a policy of repressing them—especially those from France. The secret police, always active, were specially charged with rooting out seditious thought. Even though serfdom was wrong, abolishing it would weaken Russia, and that could not be allowed. Actually, Catherine's additions of new land brought additional serfs, so that there were more serfs in Russia at the end of her reign than at the beginning.

Helping Catherine deal with all these problems—wars, rebellions, expansion—was the nobleman Grigory Potemkin. Grigory Orlov and Grigory Potemkin were the two men in her life she loved most, and neither was content with the tame life of the court. Each craved a life of achievement, and Catherine was wise enough to let them pursue fame even though it meant losing their companionship. Orlov found his fame in war. Potemkin was also a member of one of the guard regiments that helped put Catherine on the throne, but his major accomplishment was in government. And in the curious way fame works, he is most remembered for a fraud he never perpetrated and as the illicit lover of the empress he almost certainly married.

Potemkin was ten years younger than Catherine. He had joined the guards after being expelled from the University of Moscow for not attending lectures. That did not mean he did not desire an education. On the contrary, he was always asking questions, learning about the subjects

*Grigory Potemkin was one of the most capable of the noblemen who helped
Catherine expand the boundaries of the Russian Empire.*
New York Public Library Picture Collection

that interested him. He was tall, strong, good-looking, fun-loving, a
welcome guest at the parties he adored. He was well known for his
ability to imitate people. When he was first presented to Catherine, she
asked him about his imitations. Instantly he replied in the empress's
own voice, even keeping her slight German accent. While the onlookers
gasped, Catherine laughed in delight. Not long after that he made other
bold bids for royal attention, with the result that Grigory and Aleksey
Orlov beat him up. He was not intimidated. Catherine gave him some
government appointments, and then he went to fight the Turks. In
January 1774, Catherine's affair with Orlov having ended, she summoned
Potemkin back to court. In March he became her new favorite.

In spite of the difference in their ages theirs was a genuine and
heartfelt love, based on more than physical attraction. They shared a
devotion to the country Catherine had adopted, a vision of what it could
become, and the energy and intelligence to make that vision reality.

There is good evidence that they were married before a few witnesses at the end of the year 1774. Catherine thought it better not to announce her marriage, possibly remembering that Peter the Great was secretly married to his second wife for four years before he announced it.

Potemkin was glad to help Catherine rule. When she wrote decrees he corrected her mistakes in Russian grammar and spelling. He also offered much advice on policy, which she accepted if she agreed with it. For instance, King George III of England asked to hire some of her troops to help his redcoats squelch the American Revolution. Potemkin favored the idea, but Catherine refused.

A major objective at the time was to establish good government in all the provinces of Russia, including those newly added. When Potemkin grew restless at court Catherine proposed that he take charge of developing the Black Sea areas yielded by the Turks. They both saw this as a way of self-realization for him. Potemkin accepted the assignment, and Catherine sadly said farewell.

The work suited Potemkin. Twelve years later he suggested that Catherine celebrate her twenty-fifth year as empress by making a royal tour of the south. With a large company Catherine traveled down the Dnieper River from Kiev to the Black Sea in galleys Potemkin had built. She visited a modern new port and shipyards and was present for the launching of two ships.

She traveled on to the Crimean Peninsula. The new port there, Sevastopol, was even more impressive. Always dramatic, Potemkin chose carefully the house she stayed in, and at a signal a curtain on a window was opened, giving a view of a fleet of warships, which immediately fired a cannon salute to the empress. Dinner featured wines from grapes he had introduced. Fireworks followed, and on a nearby mountain the first letter of the empress's name was outlined in fifty-five thousand lights.

Potemkin showed Catherine the villages he had built for the thousands of immigrants who had come from German states to farm this land by the Black Sea. Hearing of all this, the ambassador of Saxony in Saint Petersburg attempted to discredit Potemkin by spreading a story that those villages were only a series of stage sets. The happy farmers were actors moved from place to place ahead of the tour, he claimed. Because many people were jealous of Potemkin's favored status, they repeated these charges, and they won a place in the record. But the best authorities say Potemkin's achievements were very real. So what if he built some houses specifically for his empress? Any city improves itself before playing host to a royal visit—or to today's equivalent, the Olympic Games.

On the way back to Saint Petersburg Catherine stopped at Poltava, where Potemkin staged a reenactment of Peter the Great's most famous victory. The anniversary tour lasted three months, and Catherine loved it.

In the last years of her life Catherine kept her remarkable energy. She wrote her memoirs. She commissioned a noted linguist to draw up a dictionary that would compare all the languages of the world, and took part in the research herself, writing to her fellow rulers to ask their help. She wanted to obtain American Indian words. Since George III had lost his North American colonies by then, she wrote to the marquis de Lafayette. Lafayette passed the request along to George Washington, who passed it along to one of his officers. In time Washington sent a list to Lafayette, writing "I heartily wish the attempt of that singular great character, the Empress of Russia, to form a universal dictionary, may be attended with the merited success." And in fact it was a pioneering work in the field.

Catherine was interested in more than words from North America. She sent explorers to Alaska and established a permanent colony there to collect the valuable furs of sea otters and seals.

She continued her day-by-day care for the details of government, the care that earned her reputation as a good ruler. Russia's future was much on her mind always. Her son, Paul, had three sons, Alexander, Constantine, and Nicholas, so the Romanov succession seemed assured. In 1796, at age sixty-seven, Catherine died.

CHAPTER THREE

ALEXANDER I
SAVES EUROPE

WHEN CATHERINE THE GREAT DIED IN 1796 HER SON PAUL became czar. At that time the whole world was undergoing great changes, as the result of three great revolutions. The Industrial Revolution was moving millions of people from farms to factories, and to the cities that grew up around those factories. The American Revolution had cast off the rule of the British king George III, and his former colonists were trying out a republican form of government. The French Revolution had beheaded King Louis XVI, and Frenchmen were killing each other in violent struggles over the shape a new government should take.

As always the changes reached Russia slowly. In industry, the number of Russian factories was increasing, but most were small operations, and only a tiny fraction of the population worked in them. The new American republic had sent a diplomat, Francis Dana, to Saint Petersburg in 1781, but Catherine had not received him or recognized his revolutionary government. (Dana was accompanied by fourteen-year-old John Quincy Adams of Massachusetts, who served as his secretary. Twenty-eight years later, in 1809, President James Madison would send Adams back to Saint Petersburg.)

For Czar Paul, the most important revolution was the French one. Napoléon Bonaparte was now leading the armies of France. In 1799

Napoléon would become master of the French government as well. The general explained in a metaphor: "I saw the crown of France lying in a Paris gutter. I picked it up on the point of my sword." He seemed determined to rule the whole continent of Europe. While Paul's mother, Catherine, was expanding Russia's boundaries, the European power structure had been basically stable. From south to north, the great powers were the Ottoman Empire, Austria, Prussia, France, and Great Britain. Napoléon was destroying that stability.

When Russia's neighbors Austria and Prussia joined with Great Britain to oppose Napoléon, Paul sent troops to fight beside them. To Paul's disgust the Russian troops were not welcomed. Paul's motives were questioned. The Europeans feared he was seeking to expand Russia still farther into Europe. Paul recalled his troops and opened negotiations with Napoléon—a change very unpopular with the many Russians who were carrying on profitable trade with Britain.

Paul also made many enemies by revoking a number of the government policies of Catherine that he considered too liberal. Paul's ideas on government were much more conservative than his mother's. Catherine had recognized his conservative tendencies and in her last years had turned her attention to developing her grandson, Paul's son Alexander, into a liberal ruler in her tradition. In 1800 Paul ordered an insane and disastrous military expedition to conquer India. Paul's enemies went to twenty-three-year-old Alexander and suggested they would like to overthrow Paul and make Alexander czar. Alexander, remembering his grandmother's plans for Russia, agreed, provided his father not be hurt. But Paul's enemies knew from history that it would be dangerous to have a former czar alive. They soon announced that Czar Paul had died of apoplexy. The French statesman Talleyrand, remembering that apoplexy was also the alleged cause of the death of Czar Peter III, remarked, "Really, the Russian government will have to invent another disease." Alexander was crowned Czar Alexander I in 1801.

The new czar restored many of Catherine's policies that his father had revoked. Alexander went further than Catherine had in the matter of the serfs, abolishing serfdom in the provinces along the Baltic Sea and granting permission to landowners elsewhere to release their serfs and give them enough land to live on. (Not surprisingly, few landowners did that.) Alexander commissioned yet another study of how the structure of government could be improved, perhaps even with the addition of a written constitution.

Alexander continued his grandmother's policy of expansion in the south, taking land on the shores of the Black Sea from Persia and Turkey. And in the interest of expanding foreign trade he invited President James Madison to send a diplomatic representative to Russia.

When Madison's choice, John Quincy Adams, arrived in Saint Petersburg in 1809, Alexander received him cordially. The handsome sovereign, thirty-two years old, also paid considerable attention to Adams's beautiful and witty wife, Louisa, and her equally attractive sister, Catherine, who accompanied her. The czar made known his wish that the three Americans be included in the many parties given by members of the court. The brilliant social life of the city put a painful strain on the pocketbook of Adams, brought up in the Puritan traditions of Massachusetts, but he knew dinners and balls were essential parts of diplomacy.

Adams and Alexander both took morning walks along the banks of the Neva River, even in winter weather. In February 1810 they exchanged brief greetings as they walked. Over the next two years they met often and developed a genuine friendship. One of the matters they discussed was the major concern of the entire continent: that all-conquering Frenchman, Napoléon.

Napoléon requested that Alexander close his ports to trade with Great Britain, the Frenchman's most stubborn foe, and the czar agreed. The British trade was important to Russian merchants, and that agreement was often ignored by Alexander's subjects. Napoléon made a similar request concerning trade with America. In addition Napoléon, like Alexander, wanted land on the shores of the Black Sea. Before long it became obvious that French and Russian ambitions were incompatible. In June 1812 Napoléon led an army of six hundred thousand men across the Russian border and headed for Moscow, 550 miles to the east.

Napoléon expected to fight and defeat the czar's armies in a series of set battles, march to Moscow, and add Russia to his long list of conquered nations. But Russian strategy was quite different from what he had encountered elsewhere. When Napoléon's troops approached a Russian position, the Russian troops inflicted what casualties they could and then retreated, avoiding a major battle and preserving their numbers. Between these encounters, skillful cossack horsemen carried out hit-and-run attacks on the invaders. The result was a steady reduction of Napoléon's troop strength.

By September the invaders had reached a point seventy miles southeast of Moscow. The Russians chose a site near the village of Borodino to make a stand at last. The Battle of Borodino, fought on September 7, 1812, is considered by the Russians a turning point in Napoléon's career. Attacks and counterattacks produced heavy casualties on both sides. Napoléon, suffering from a fever, lacked his customary decisiveness and held some of his best troops in reserve throughout the day. By nightfall the Russians had not defeated him, but they had denied him the clearcut victory he sought.

The Russians again withdrew, leaving the road to Moscow open. Napoléon entered the city unopposed on September 14. He found that most of the population had fled. A few days later the city was on fire, burned by the Russians to destroy the food and shelter the French needed for the approaching winter. Napoléon, like Charles XII of Sweden a century earlier, found himself a long way from home, with no way to get supplies. The invasion of Russia was the greatest mistake of Napoléon's life, one from which he never recovered. He had no choice but to lead his army back out of Russia. John Quincy Adams wrote in his memoirs: "From Moscow to Prussia, 800 miles of road have been strewed with his artillery, baggage, wagons, ammunition chests, dead and dying men, whom he has been forced to abandon to their fate. . . . The two Russian generals who have conquered Napoléon and all his Marshalls are *General Famine* and *General Frost*." The Russians repeatedly harassed the retreat. But more men succumbed to the bitter cold and to illness than to swords or bullets. Less than a sixth of the six hundred thousand invaders reached home. Peter Ilich Tchaikovsky, born a generation later, celebrated the defeat of the French in his "1812 Overture," scored for symphony orchestra and cannons.

Now the armies of Russia, Great Britain, Prussia, Spain, and Sweden combined to bring about Napoléon's final defeat. Alexander personally led the victors into Paris. He was regarded as the savior of the continent and played a leading role in the peace talks that followed, called the Congress of Vienna. The Treaty of Paris that the Congress drew up, signed in 1815, gave to Russia Finland, part of Poland, and more land by the Black Sea. More important, the victory over Napoléon meant

In 1812 Napoléon Bonaparte attempted to extend his conquest of Europe into Russia and there met the defeat that led to his downfall three years later.

*Peter Ilich Tchaikovsky composed symphonies, operas, ballet music,
and concertos that are still popular around the world.*
Library of Congress

Czar Alexander began going to "summit meetings" of European sovereigns. Most important, in the long run, the Russians who fought in Europe acquired a personal acquaintance with countries they had only heard about before. Many of them liked what they saw—especially the status and living conditions of ordinary people in Europe. They compared independent European farmers with the serfs in Russia. The better educated among the Russian officers recognized that the principles advocated by the thinkers of the eighteenth-century Enlightenment were being put into practice, with good results. Some of these men resolved to work for change in ancient Mother Russia.

Surprisingly, the Russians most active in bringing about change in the nineteenth century belonged to noble families—families that would lose some of their wealth in a new social order. They were young men, with the idealism of youth and the leisure to debate political ideas. Many of them joined reform societies, which met in secret. (Catherine had taught Alexander liberal ideas, but she had also taught him to be very

protective of royal power, and political discussions were closely monitored.) These young men were called "Pugachovs of the academies" after
Yemelyan Pugachov, the most important rebel leader of Catherine's reign.
They looked for ways to bring about long-discussed reforms, including
a written constitution for the nation.

In 1825 Czar Alexander died. He had no sons to succeed him, so
his younger brother Nicholas was crowned czar in December of that
year. On Sunday, December 14, thirty young army officers and three
thousand soldiers demonstrated in Saint Petersburg in support of a
constitution. Nicholas sent loyal regiments and the military governor of
the city out to persuade the men to disperse, and a young officer shot
and killed the governor. When many civilians began to join the protest,
Nicholas's regiments opened fire on the demonstrators with artillery,
killing more than seventy of them. The leaders of the demonstration
were tried; five were executed and many more were exiled. The incident,
given the name the Decembrist Revolt, had gotten Nicholas's reign off
to a terrible start.

Nicholas had not had the benefit of the instruction Catherine gave
his brother Alexander. The Decembrist Revolt had frightened him badly.
As a result he ordered strict repression by the secret police of political
discussion. But Nicholas did recognize there were improvements needed.
Like most new rulers he set up new commissions to study and make
recommendations. Areas to be considered were finance, government
structure, education, religion, and that constant nagging question, what
to do about the serfs.

The "Pugachovs of the academies" did not expect the new commissions to accomplish much more than the earlier ones. Their own efforts
were closely watched, lectures were monitored, and political publications
were censored. But a new method of spreading their thoughts developed:
the writing of poems, plays, and novels. In eighteenth-century Europe
novels had enjoyed enormous popularity for the good stories they told.
In the nineteenth century a new kind of literature appeared, the "novel
of ideas," which used a story to stimulate the reader's thinking about
important issues. Nowhere was the novel of ideas developed more successfully than in Russia.

Nikolay Gogol wrote a brilliant attack on corruption in his novel
Dead Souls and portrayed the widespread bribery of officials in his comic
play *The Inspector General*. Mikhail Lermontov chose as the central char-

*Nevsky Prospect, the main street of Saint Petersburg, as it looked
in the middle of the nineteenth century*
Library of Congress

acter of his novel *A Hero of Our Times* a man who feels his life is wasted
because he is required to spend it as an army officer. Russia's most
beloved poet, Aleksandr Pushkin, also portrayed men frustrated in their
aspirations by the demands of the state, in such narrative poems as
Eugene Onegin and *The Bronze Horseman*. A generation later Ivan Tur-
genev portrayed the bitter life of the serfs in his collection of stories *A
Sportsman's Sketches*. Still later a Saint Petersburg physician, Anton
Chekhov, brilliantly depicted the lives of the country gentry in such
plays as *The Cherry Orchard* and *The Three Sisters*.

In the middle of the nineteenth century Russia produced two of the
greatest novelists of any time or place. Their works had enormous influence both on political thought and on world literature. One was
Fyodor Dostoyevsky, author of *Crime and Punishment* and *The Brothers
Karamazov*, unforgettable explorations of the possibilities of the human

Leo Tolstoy, author of War and Peace, *although a nobleman, spent the last years of his life working to improve the plight of the people.*
Library of Congress

spirit. The other was Leo Tolstoy, a Russian count who felt great concern for the ordinary people of Russia. He freed the serfs on his estates and established progressive schools for their children. His masterpieces are *Anna Karenina*, a portrait of a woman seeking the true meaning of love, and his epic account of Russia at the time of Napoléon's invasion, *War and Peace.*

For all their greatness, for all their success in stimulating thought and discussion about the state of society, these Russian writers had few specific remedies to propose. In Germany and Great Britain, where industrial development was more advanced than anywhere else, and therefore workers' problems were more severe, three men did offer solutions. All three concentrated on the conditions of factory workers.

The first of these men, a German, expected nothing but a worsening of the workers' plight until the workers themselves took steps to change conditions. He felt conflict between workers and factory owners was inevitable, and the only solution was for the workers to seize ownership for themselves. Because he advocated that the property seized be held by all the workers in common, his ideas were given the name *communism*. His name was Karl Marx. The second man was Marx's close friend, Friedrich Engels. Together they wrote a pamphlet expounding their ideas, entitled *The Communist Manifesto*. It was published in 1848.

The third man with a remedy was the British owner of a number of cotton mills in Manchester, Robert Owen. He saw the hardships all the mill workers had to endure and set about improving conditions, first for his own employees and then for all workers. He campaigned successfully in Great Britain for a law that would regulate the number of hours worked and the employment of children. He developed a complete community for his workers in Great Britain and later established in the United States the town of New Harmony, Indiana, where his theories could be tried out. Owen's ideas for social change were the first to be given the name *socialism*. Later socialists had more far-reaching ideas for change, advocating not only government regulation but government ownership of industry, brought about by peaceful democratic processes.

Neither Marx nor Engels nor Owen dreamed that their ideas would have their most complete test in a country much less industrialized than Germany or Great Britain: the Russia of the next century.

CZAR NICHOLAS I, LIKE ALEXANDER I, MET WITH HIS FELLOW sovereigns in Europe, and for a time relations were good. Nicholas squelched a revolt in Poland and helped the Austrian emperor put down one in Hungary, earning for himself the nickname Gendarme of Europe.

At this time the Turkish Ottoman Empire, which had ruled most of the eastern end of the Mediterranean Sea for centuries, stretched all the way to the Danube River, its border with Austria-Hungary. But it was growing weak. All the great powers saw in that weakness an opportunity to acquire some desirable territories. Czar Nicholas often raised the question of action against Turkey, a nation he called "the sick man of Europe." But the other powers gave him no encouragement, afraid once again of Russian expansion. Nicholas then declared that he had a responsibility as a Christian ruler to protect the Christians living under the rule of Muslims in the Ottoman Empire and in 1853 sent his armies into two Turkish provinces near the Danube River. At that point Turkey declared war. Great Britain and France, distrusting Nicholas's motives and jealous of their own interests in the eastern Mediterranean, also declared war on Russia. Nicholas's armies were driven back. Moreover, the British and French decided to try to destroy the Russian Black Sea naval base at Sevastopol, the port Grigory Potemkin had developed for Catherine at the tip of the Crimean Peninsula. History calls the hostilities that followed the Crimean War.

British ships landed an expeditionary force on the peninsula to lay siege to Sevastopol. The city was well fortified and held out for 349 days, falling at last because its location made it difficult to get supplies and reinforcements to it, and because of bureaucratic bungling. Count Leo Tolstoy, not yet a famous writer, was among the defenders and won great acclaim for his account, *The Tales of Sevastopol*. And at Balaklava a British cavalry unit won lasting fame through Alfred Lord Tennyson's poem "The Charge of the Light Brigade," containing these wry lines:

> *Theirs not to reason why,*
> *Theirs but to do and die:*
> *Into the valley of Death*
> *Rode the six hundred.*

Final victory when it came was far from glorious for the invaders. Their troops had suffered terrible hardships. The only positive result of the Crimean War was the achievement of an English woman, Florence Nightingale. She succeeded in badgering her government into providing better nursing care for wounded and ill soldiers.

While the siege was in progress Czar Nicholas died. His son was crowned Alexander II, and he immediately began peace negotiations, which led to another Treaty of Paris in 1856. The Black Sea was declared neutral waters, to be kept free of both Russian and Turkish military bases and the warships of all nations. That seemed like a good plan, if everyone kept the treaty provisions.

•   •   •

Czar Alexander II made few attempts to extend his boundaries westward into Europe. Instead he looked east and south. He joined with other European nations in extracting concessions in Asia from the Chinese Empire, once mighty but now weakened by rebellion and corruption. He pushed the boundary of Siberia south to the Amur and Ussuri rivers. At the southern tip of his new Pacific coastline Alexander established a port that would be free of ice and usable all year long. Alexander named the port Vladivostok, Russian for "Lord of the East." (His son began construction of a railroad to connect Moscow and Russia's interior with that port, across the vastness of Siberia. When it was completed, the Trans-Siberian Railroad was the longest track project in the world, 5,542 miles long.)

Only nineteen miles from Siberia's coast was the tip of the Aleutian Island chain, a part of the Russian colony in Alaska, established by Catherine the Great in 1784. Alaska had produced wonderful furs for the nobles in Saint Petersburg, and in 1812 Russians had established another fur-trading post farther down the coast at Fort Ross, just north of San Francisco Bay. But the Russian colonies in America did not prosper for long. Neglected by Catherine's successors, the colonists had gone their own way, greedily hunting the seals and otters almost to extinction. As a result, by the time of Alexander II, Alaska was producing nothing of value for Russia.

The political situation in North America had also changed. San Francisco Bay and the whole territory of California had been acquired by the United States from Mexico in 1848. The British had pushed their settlement of Canada to the Pacific. American and British interests were prospering along the Pacific coast. If their westward expansion meant either Britain or the United States wanted Alaska, Alexander saw no reason to fight to keep it. This young American republic had a novel approach to acquiring territory, however. Instead of invading it, Americans sometimes bought it. When Napoléon Bonaparte was hard-pressed for funds in 1807, he had sold France's huge colony of Louisiana to the Americans for $15 million. The czar's government was always hard-pressed for funds. Alexander requested his diplomats to find out, discreetly, if the Americans would like to buy Alaska.

The Americans just then were intensely occupied with internal affairs, debating issues that would soon provoke a terrible civil war. They were not interested in talking about Alaska. But when the Civil War began, they conducted a secret negotiation that has only recently been brought to light. Great Britain seemed likely to support the Southern states in order to protect the supply of their cotton for her textile mills. Planners in Washington wondered if British ships might make trouble along the Pacific coast of the United States. It would be a great comfort to have the Russian czar oppose such action. American and Russian diplomats agreed that if Czar Alexander would maintain peace in the Pacific, President Lincoln would buy Alaska once the Civil War was won. In 1863 the czar sent a Russian fleet to San Francisco Bay and another into New York Harbor to show his sympathy for the Union cause. Lincoln did not live to see the agreement kept. But in 1867, two years after the war was over, the United States bought Alaska, with its enormous mineral wealth, from Russia for $7.2 million.

IN THE SOUTHWESTERN CORNER OF HIS EMPIRE Czar Alexander brought under Russian control the lands east and west of the Caspian Sea. West of the Caspian rise the Caucasus Mountains, including Mount Elbrus, the highest peak in Europe. Three kingdoms shared the land between the Black Sea and the Caspian: Armenia, Georgia, and Azerbaijan. For centuries the three had fought to maintain their independence against invaders from Persia to the south and Russia to the north. No conqueror had permanently overcome their fierce fighters, who knew how to use the mountainous terrain to defeat conventional armies. But one of Alexander's generals did force the surrender of the strongest Georgian chief and eventually put an end to fighting in the area.

East of the Caspian the Russians had founded a number of towns, but they were frequently raided by the native inhabitants of the region. A Russian statesman compared the situation to the Indian raids on the American frontier. The natives had resisted for centuries all efforts of the czars to control them, in part because they were followers of the Muslim religion, and mainly because they loved their independence. Alexander sent his modern armies against them, captured their cities, including Samarkand and Tashkent, and forced their leaders to accept his government. He continued pressing south until his troops reached the foothills of the Himalayas and the border of Afghanistan.

South of the Himalayas another sovereign, Queen Victoria, had added the subcontinent of India to the British Empire. The world's highest mountain range now separated two great empires, both expanding. Alexander's statesmen suggested that Afghanistan be left as a buffer state between them. That is to say, any hostile action by either would be absorbed by the small buffer nation, giving the other great power time to decide how to respond. But fear of Russian expansion had been strong in Britain since the time of Catherine the Great. The British thought India would be safer if Britain had unquestioned control of Afghanistan. They invaded from India and dictated the choice of a king, and Alexander did not challenge that outcome. (British control lasted until 1921, when an independent government was established.)

Expanding Russian territory was important. But Alexander II is better remembered for his accomplishments in improving life for his people. During his reign the number of elementary schools in Russia grew from eight thousand to twenty-three thousand. Secondary education was opened to anyone who could pass an entrance examination. Higher education was opened to women. Alexander relaxed censorship, at least for a time. The system of trial by jury was introduced for the first time, supplementing trial by a judge alone.

Most important, Alexander II was the czar who finally abolished serfdom. His father had made him a member of the commission to study that perennial question. There were no simple answers. A family of serfs had to earn a living somehow. Most were farmers. (Czar Alexander I had granted "permission" to the landowners to give the serfs land to live on, an unrealistic approach.) Furthermore, serfs would need some form of local government to replace rule by the landowners. Alexander II, in a complicated set of acts, emancipated the serfs and set up village governments. Ownership of a portion of the land formerly worked by the serfs was transferred to the villages. The landowners were compensated for the land by the nation. The nation, in turn, was to be compensated by the villages, with payment spread over the next forty-nine years. The date was 1861, two years before President Abraham Lincoln signed the Emancipation Proclamation freeing the slaves in the United States.

No one was satisfied with the details of Alexander's plan. In many areas the serfs found the village-owned land was inadequate to grow enough food to feed their families. The landowners had lost the labor of their serfs and had also lost some of their power in local government. Political societies in the cities discussed dozens of theories on how the

For centuries the nobles controlled the lives of the serfs. The bitter title of this painting is The Landlord Exchanging People for Dogs.
New York Public Library Picture Collection

emancipation could be improved. Alexander attempted adjustments for many years, but discontent continued. Riots occurred often, as well as acts of violence by individuals or small groups protesting government decisions or policies.

Some of the protests were planned by leaders who advocated doing away with government altogether. The goal of these leaders was *anarchy*, a word taken from the Greek for "no government." They believed that mankind, freed of government compulsion, could live in perfect harmony, owning all property in common, as proposed by thinkers from Plato to Karl Marx. One of their methods to achieve that end more quickly was assassination of heads of state. (The man who assassinated U.S. president William McKinley had such beliefs.) For their beliefs they were called *anarchists*; for their methods they were called *terrorists*.

A favorite weapon of a terrorist was a homemade bomb. Czar Alexander, as head of the government, was a prime target. One bomb was placed under a railroad track he was to travel, but it blew up the train before his. Another bomb blew up his dinner table minutes before he

55

*After many attempts, in 1881 the revolutionaries succeeded in
assassinating Czar Alexander II by blowing up his carriage.*
National Archives

arrived for dinner. As a result of these and other attempts on his life,
he returned to some of the repression practiced by his father following
the Decembrist Revolt in 1825. But in 1881, on the very day he signed
a paper that he considered a first step toward a written constitution for
Russia, a bomb thrown at his carriage succeeded in ending his life.

The son of Alexander II was crowned Alexander III. His first act was
to tear up the paper concerning a constitution. The action was indicative
of his intentions. He ruled for thirteen years, always trying to restore to

the landowners the influence they had lost under Alexander II and to root out the revolutionary ideas that were being discussed in Russia. He was too late. He could not give the landowners back their serfs. He could execute men advocating revolution, but he could not kill their ideas.

Most significantly, Alexander III executed a young man named Ulyanov, a member of an unsuccessful assassination plot. That execution set the course of the life of Ulyanov's seventeen-year-old younger brother, who became the most effective leader the revolutionary movement ever had. To elude the czar's police that brother, Vladimir Ilich Ulyanov, changed his name from Ulyanov to Lenin.

CHAPTER FOUR

LENIN VERSUS ROMANOV

VLADIMIR ILICH ULYANOV, ALIAS V. I. LENIN, WAS BORN in 1870 in Simbirsk, a small city on the Volga River about 450 miles east of Moscow. His father was an educator who was made director of education for the province when Vladimir was four years old. That was an important post and carried with it the title of "hereditary nobleman in the service of the czar." Learning was naturally emphasized in the Ulyanov family, and all the children did well in school. Vladimir's older brother, Aleksandr, went to Saint Petersburg to study at the university there. Vladimir was especially strong in languages, learning to read Latin, Greek, French, and German. He was always at the top of his class, and when he took the exams at seventeen that would admit him to a university, he earned the highest possible grade, five, in every subject except logic. In logic he earned a four. He was admitted to the University of Kazan, where his father had studied. He intended to become a laywer.

That same year, when Vladimir was seventeen, there occurred the events that were to change the course of his life forever. His older brother joined a group of young men in Saint Petersburg who plotted to assassinate Czar Alexander III. The plot, organized by amateurs, failed miserably, and the conspirators were arrested. Vladimir's brother and four others were hanged.

*A school photo of Vladimir Ulyanov, who took the name Lenin after he became
actively involved in plans to overthrow the Czar's government*
Library of Congress

Vladimir entered the University of Kazan as he had planned. It was
a troubled year for students in Russia. When the czar's minister of
education began to clamp down on their political activities, protests
broke out all over the nation. When Vladimir attended a mass meeting
of students, the police recognized him as the brother of a convicted
revolutionary and arrested him along with thirty-nine others. He was
released after three days but was expelled from the university.

He returned to his family and began to study law on his own. Four
years later he obtained permission to take the examinations for a law
degree. He took them at the University of Saint Petersburg and received
the top grade of the 124 candidates. It was clear he was more than just

a good student. His brilliant mind was paired with a remarkable determination to overcome obstacles put in his way.

He practiced law in his home province for two years, but his mind was on the affairs of the nation. For in the years that he was studying his law books he was also thinking about what had happened to his brother. He read many criticisms of the czar's government. And he read with great care Karl Marx's book *Capital*, with its warning that in industrial societies a few rich owners—capitalists—were acquiring a larger and larger share of all wealth, leaving less and less for working people. Lenin believed that *The Communist Manifesto* written by Marx and Engels contained answers for the ills of the world, Russia included. He began to write his own criticisms, phrased in the strongest sort of language. He published them under various pseudonyms to avoid further arrests.

When Vladimir was twenty-three he went back to Saint Petersburg to support himself by working in a law office while he joined the struggle for a new Russia. His keen mind, caustic pen, and sharp tongue quickly earned him a welcome among the reformers in the capital. One of them was a young woman, Nadezhda Krupskaya, who was to become his lifelong partner in marriage and in revolution.

In 1895 Vladimir, who now called himself V. I. Lenin, and other reform leaders arranged the merger of about twenty small groups in Saint Petersburg to form the Fighting Union of the Working Class. For that work Vladimir Lenin was sentenced to three years exile in Siberia.

The exile was a relatively mild sentence, requiring Lenin to live in a small town in southern Siberia but leaving him free to do as he pleased. Nadezhda Krupskaya was also exiled. She joined Lenin, and they were married. Lenin actually gained weight in exile. He also grew a beard, perhaps hoping to compensate for the premature loss of most of the hair on his head. The beard was bright red, and his appearance, a bald young man with a red beard, made him immediately recognizable. He spent most of his time in Siberia writing, and when the three years ended he voluntarily left Russia to work with other revolutionaries in various European cities including Munich, London, and Geneva. These men and women had a goal of an international revolution that would put an end to capitalism everywhere. For the Russians among them, the first step was the overthrow of the czar. Lenin's passionate words on revolution were widely read. He was recognized more and more as a leader of the revolutionaries.

MEANWHILE, IN 1898, IN RUSSIA, A SMALL MEETING OF TEN delegates from workers' organizations in four cities founded the Russian Social Democratic Labor party. That party became in time the Communist party of the Soviet Union, but in 1898 it was only one of many organizations working for government reform. Its second meeting was held outside Russia, in Brussels, Belgium, to avoid the czar's secret police. When the Belgian police objected, the delegates moved to London. Lenin was present. It was clear that he intended to have his ideas on revolution adopted as the platform of the party. A violent debate took place— Lenin's language was never moderate. Neither were his ideas. He advocated that membership in the party be limited to a small group of "expert revolutionaries" who would direct the workers in the overthrow of the czar and then set up a dictatorship to rule the country. Other delegates favored a more democratic course, with party membership open to all.

The meeting voted in favor of Lenin's ideas by a narrow majority. But the vote split the party into minority and majority factions. In Russian, minority and majority are *menshevik* and *bolshevik*. After that vote Lenin and his followers were known as Bolsheviks. For the next fifteen years they would plan and work and sometimes fight to overthrow the government of the czar.

CZAR ALEXANDER III HAD DIED OF NATURAL CAUSES AT THE early age of forty-nine, in 1894. His son was crowned Nicholas II. The new ruler was twenty-six, only two years older than the young revolutionary Lenin. He had expected to have many more years as a carefree prince before the responsibilities of government settled on his shoulders. He had had a good education by a tutor and had done particularly well in the study of religion and languages. His family was a truly international one. His mother was a Danish princess. His wife's grandmother was Queen Victoria, crowned in 1837 and still the most powerful monarch of the day. Two of his English cousins were to become King Edward VII and King George V. Another cousin was Kaiser Wilhelm of Germany. The European practice of strengthening treaties and alliances through royal marriages was still very much alive.

Czar Nicholas II and his cousin King George V of England
Library of Congress

Royal cousins were a great help for Czar Nicholas in international relations. He proposed that the European nations hold a conference to seek ways to insure peace, and all his cousins agreed to send delegates, although some thought the idea foolishly idealistic.

The International Peace Conference that Czar Nicholas II proposed met at The Hague in Holland in 1899. It established the International Court of Justice that still hears claims between nations today. While the delegates were meeting, a new threat to peace was developing in Russia's vast neighbor, China. The Empress Dowager Tz'u-hsi, who had dominated the government for thirty-eight years, had not been able to prevent foreign commercial interests from gaining enormous influence in China. Now an organization of militant Chinese, the Society of the Righteous Fists, nicknamed the Boxers, had adopted the slogan Throw the Foreign Devils Out. Boxer leaders recruited an army and laid siege to the capital, Beijing. The Empress Dowager and her nephew the emperor fled the city. Foreign diplomats in the city telegraphed urgent appeals for protection to their governments, and sixteen nations sent a joint expeditionary force to Beijing. The diplomats were saved after a siege of fifty-five days, and the Boxer Rebellion was over.

Russian diplomats were among those threatened by the Boxers, but Czar Nicholas had another reason for sending soldiers to China. The part of China that interested him most was the province of Manchuria, near Russia's new port on the Pacific, Vladivostok. The Trans-Siberian Railway was being built from Moscow toward this port, and the shortest route would be across Manchuria. Vladivostok was free of ice except in the coldest months. Farther south, Manchuria had an even better port, always ice free. In 1898 Russian diplomats had arranged to lease that port from China, and Russia had built there a naval base called Port Arthur. While Tz'u-hsi was busy with the Boxers, Russian soldiers moved into Manchuria.

Another nation much concerned with what happened in Manchuria was Japan. The Japanese had their eyes on the great natural resources of that province. Japanese diplomats in Saint Petersburg demanded the withdrawal of the Russian troops. Negotiations were broken off in February 1904, and two days later the Japanese navy, without warning, attacked Russian ships at anchor at the Port Arthur naval base. Two days after that Japan and Russia declared war. (Comparison is unavoidable with the events surrounding the Japanese attack on the American base at Pearl Harbor on December 7, 1941.)

To the amazement of the world, and the humiliation of Nicholas, little Japan proceeded to defeat vast Russia in every battle. Russia's vastness was the very problem. Supplies for Russian soldiers had to be transported thousands of miles overland, while supplies for Japanese troops arrived easily by ship. Port Arthur fell in December 1904 after a two-month siege. In February 1905 the Russian and Japanese armies met near the Manchurian city of Mukden. Four hundred thousand Japanese faced nearly as many Russians—numbers surpassing all others in the history of warfare to that time. The battle lasted three weeks and

In 1904 the Japanese launched a surprise attack on Russian warships in the harbor of Port Arthur, Manchuria, and sank these two.
Library of Congress

ended in defeat for the Russians, with tens of thousands of casualties for both sides.

Reinforcements for the Russian Far East Fleet had left Saint Petersburg on a journey that took seven months. They had to travel around Europe and Africa and much of Asia to reach the Straits of Tsushima, between Japan and the mainland. There, on May 27, 1905, the Japanese fleet engaged them in battle and in two days destroyed all but four of the forty Russian ships that had completed the long voyage.

Now both Russia and Japan were ready for peace. The president of the United States, Theodore Roosevelt, arranged a peace conference at Portsmouth, New Hampshire. By the Treaty of Portsmouth, Russia transferred to Japan the lease on Port Arthur and other rights in Manchuria, in effect giving Japan the domination she sought.

All during the Russo-Japanese War bad news from the front fueled criticism at home of Nicholas's government. Student protests increased. Workers went on strike. Lenin printed a newspaper in Geneva that was smuggled into Russia.

In January 1905 a leader of the workers in Saint Petersburg suggested a peaceful demonstration at the Winter Palace. They would present a petition to Czar Nicholas asking for election of a parliament, amnesty for political prisoners, a minimum wage, better working conditions, and other reforms. On Sunday, January 9, thousands of workers marched toward the palace carrying flags, banners with slogans, and portraits of the czar. But the czar's ministers did not trust the peaceful intentions of the organizers and did not consult Nicholas, who was at another palace outside the city. Instead, they sent troops to block the march. The workers, eager to see their "father czar," pushed forward anyway, the troops fired into the crowd, and more than a hundred demonstrators were killed. A day that began in hope had become "Bloody Sunday."

Nicholas was horrified when he learned what had happened. He tried to make amends by meeting with a small delegation of workers. But it did no good. News of the killings spread, causing revolts all over the country. The sailors on the battleship *Potemkin* in the Black Sea threw their officers overboard and turned their heavy guns on towns along the shore. Assassinations by terrorists increased. Advocates of land reform adopted a new, stronger slogan: All Land to the Peasants.

In the cities the workers developed a new kind of organziation to influence the government. Workers in a particular trade elected delegates to

On Bloody Sunday, January 9, 1905, czarist troops fired on workers demonstrating for better conditions, killing more than a hundred.
Le Petit Parisien

a council, and the trade councils elected delegates to a larger council representing all trades in the city. The Russian word for council is *soviet.*

In October 1905 the railway workers in Saint Petersburg went on strike to demand a constitution, and called on all other workers to join them. The business of the nation was brought to a halt by a general strike. Nicholas could not ignore that situation and issued a decree promising freedom of speech, the press, and assembly, and summoning an elected parliament, to be called by the traditional name Duma. The Saint Petersburg soviet ended the strike. Ten days later, however, it called another strike. But this one was less effective, and Nicholas sought to reassert his authority by arresting most of the members of the soviet. They called a third strike, which also proved ineffective in Saint Petersburg. But the far-reaching power of the workers' organizations now became evident. In Moscow workers went on strike and fought with the troops who were sent to coerce them. Similar conflicts took place in various cities in the southern part of Russia.

It seemed for a few days that a struggle to overthrow the czar had begun. Lenin returned from Europe to Saint Petersburg. Then the troops overcame the workers and restored order. But Lenin said later that the efforts of 1905 were a necessary rehearsal for successful revolution.

The new Duma met the following year, as promised. It soon became clear, however, that Nicholas viewed it as merely an advisory body, with no real power. When the Duma insisted on debating such issues as the breaking up of the large estates, Nicholas adjourned it twice and revised the qualifications for membership so that landowners would have the most seats. That more conservative Duma met regularly from 1908–1917 but was far from being the freely elected legislature the reformers wanted.

THE YEAR 1905 ALSO SAW THE BEGINNING OF A FAMILY TRAGEDY for the czar. Like many Romanovs before him, Nicholas II had found his wife in one of the small German states. Her father was the grand duke of Hesse-Darmstadt, and her mother was Queen Victoria's daughter Alice. When she adopted the Russian Orthodox faith before marrying Nicholas, she took the Russian name Alexandra. And like many royal brides before her, Alexandra found it easier to change her name than to change her ideas. She and Nicholas were very much in love—he rejected two other proposed brides to marry her—but the Russian court had a morality that seemed to her very lax. She could not conceal her disapproval of women who wore dresses with revealing necklines, or of married men who openly carried on love affairs. She made few friends in Russia. Her happiest times were those spent away from Saint Peters-

Czar Nicholas II and his beautiful German wife, Alexandra
Library of Congress

burg on the czar's many royal estates, enjoying with her devoted husband their four daughters. Her favorite residence was the Alexander Palace, fifteen miles from the capital.

In August 1904 Alexandra gave birth to a fifth child, her first son. Now there was a male heir to the throne. He was welcomed with cannon salutes of three hundred guns. The child was christened Alexis.

The joy of Nicholas and Alexandra was soon darkened by the discovery that the boy had inherited from his mother's family the genetic disorder hemophilia. His blood did not clot normally, so that a simple nosebleed could be life threatening. A bump could cause a seepage of blood into tissue under the skin, which resulted in painful swelling. If the swelling affected a joint, it made it impossible to bend the joint, and the pain was intense. Because the problem is genetic there is still no cure for hemophilia. There is only therapy of massage and exercise to reduce the swellings, and whatever ways can be devised to protect the child from injuries. It is difficult to imagine what life is like for any growing boy under these conditions. And when that boy is the heir of an empire and a dynasty, the life of a whole family can easily begin to revolve around his affliction.

Certainly Alexandra's life became one long search for help for her son. The czar's mind too was never free of concern. During the recurring episodes of great pain he took turns sitting by his son's bed, listening helplessly to his pleas for relief.

Into this almost desperate situation stepped one of the strangest figures in any nation's history—a great bear of a man from Siberia named Grigory Rasputin.

Rasputin called himself a "man of God" and claimed that he could summon divine power to heal sickness. After wandering about Russia for some years he reached Saint Petersburg in his midthirties, in the year 1905. He demonstrated his healing powers to the satisfaction of many people in the capital city and was introduced at court in 1907. Some believed he was God's agent. Others thought he employed hypnotism to cure—his blue-gray eyes had an inescapable intensity. Today we know that many ailments are helped if the patient's mental state is changed. Whatever the explanation, Rasputin was able to relieve the suffering of the most important patient in Russia, the heir to the throne, Alexis. And that made Rasputin very important to the boy's parents. In

Czar Nicholas II and his son, Alexis, both in Imperial Army uniform, review a cossack regiment at the front in World War I.
Bakhmeteff Archive, Columbia University

time he replaced his Siberian rustic clothes with clothes more appropriate to royal palaces. He also acquired some royal ambitions.

In 1906, a year after Rasputin arrived in Saint Petersburg and a year after the 1905 revolution was put down, Czar Nicholas took another step toward dealing with the demands of the various political parties. He appointed a new prime minister. Peter Stolypin was a capable statesman who saw that the people of Russia had real grievances, but also saw that the terrorist tactics some were using were damaging the nation severely. First he rounded up hundreds of terrorists and executed them. Then he proposed a solution to the most pressing problem, the farmers' lack of enough land to feed their families: abandon the system set up by Alexander II for ownership of land by village councils and instead

Grigory Rasputin, a monk from Siberia, acquired great influence over the czar and his wife because he could relieve the suffering of their son.
New York Public Library Picture Collection

let the farmers own land outright. To help this idea along, Czar Nicholas gave four million acres of Romanov land to the government to be sold to the farmers, with payment spread over a period of years.

The results were good. Farmers always get better crops from land that they own. And the weather cooperated for several years. Hunger decreased. And so did revolts in the countryside. At the same time, the industrial growth that was sweeping the world at the beginning of the twentieth century was penetrating into Russia. International corporations were investing in factories in Russia. Recovery from the economic problems of a decade earlier, and from the losses of the Russo-Japanese War, seemed a real possibility.

Then two things happened to change the future. First, a terrorist assassinated Prime Minister Stolypin, and there was no minister able to continue his progressive ideas. And second, Czar Nicholas's royal cousins in Europe began to fight.

NICHOLAS'S "COUSIN WILLY," ALSO KNOWN AS KAISER Wilhelm of Germany, had urged the czar's occupation of Manchuria, which had led to the disastrous war with Japan. After that the two men were not as close to each other as in the past, even though Alexandra still entertained her many German relatives. On the other hand, Cousin George, now King George V of Great Britain, was still a welcome companion for cruises on royal yachts and games of tennis.

Both the Germans and the British were seeking to expand their influence and commercial activities in many parts of the world, and they often found themselves in direct competition. Both nations were prepared to fight if necessary to get what they wanted. They went to war over the little country of Serbia (later part of Yugoslavia). Russia was soon involved.

Serbia had broken away from the weakening Ottoman Empire and declared its independence. Czar Nicholas had promised to protect that independence—protecting at the same time Russian influence in that area. The chief threat to Serbia was Austria-Hungary next door, eager to pick up all the Ottoman land it could. A Serbian zealot protested that threat by assassinating the heir to the throne of Austria-Hungary. Austria-Hungary declared war on Serbia. Nicholas mobilized troops. Germany, also eyeing the Ottoman lands, then declared war on Russia. Britain and France, determined to prevent Germany from expanding further on the continent, declared war on Germany. The war had begun that today we call World War I.

Despite the progress that had been made in the last few years, Russia's economy was by no means ready for another war. Nevertheless, Nicholas sent to the German border millions of men—the largest army in Europe. Because he knew the soldiers regarded him as "father czar," and also because he had some of the Romanov love of soldiering, he went himself to army headquarters near the fighting. Because the name of his capital city, Saint Petersburg, had a German sound to it, he changed its name to the Russian equivalent, Petrograd.

The opposing armies pushed each other back and forth across the border. The immediate results were enormous casualties on both sides and an impossible drain on the Russian economy. The long-term result was that the Russian people lost all confidence in their czar.

While Nicholas was away with the army, back in Saint Petersburg, now Petrograd, his wife issued commands to the government, perhaps remembering she was a granddaughter of that strong-minded ruler Queen Victoria. The Russians, however, remembered Alexandra was also a daughter of a German duke and therefore possibly sympathetic to the enemy. To make matters worse, Alexandra's chief adviser was now that so-called man of God, Rasputin. His influence on the pain of Alexis was undeniably good; his influence on the commands issued by Alexandra was undeniably bad. Rasputin advised her to get rid of officials who were hostile to him and to appoint men he could control. And those men lacked the governing ability Russia desperately needed.

Alexandra, advised by Rasputin, was well on the way toward wrecking the government when a small group of men decided to put an end to Rasputin's influence and his life. One of them invited Rasputin to his house. While the others waited he fed him cake and wine liberally dosed with cyanide. To the host's horror, the poison seemed to have no effect. Rasputin called for more wine. The host then borrowed a revolver and shot him at close range. He fell but soon stood up and came charging at his assailant, who fled. Another member of the group managed to put two more bullets into Rasputin, and he fell again. The men threw what they thought was a corpse into the Neva River, but Rasputin was still alive, struggling in the water. Finally he drowned, having earned the distinction of the man who had to be killed three times, by poison, bullets, and drowning.

Rasputin was now a martyr in the eyes of Alexandra. She banished the man who had planned his murder. The czar returned to Petrograd deeply depressed by news of the war and news of the hardships the war was causing his people. But he ignored his advisers, who pointed out the effect his wife was having on the country and who warned him the people would not endure much more. By not dealing with the political situation, he gave his critics, including Lenin, the opportunity they had been waiting for.

CHAPTER FIVE

A REVOLUTION FOR "BREAD, PEACE, LAND"

In February 1917 Czar Nicholas returned to army headquarters at the front, leaving his wife, Alexandra, and the ministers chosen by Rasputin still in charge of running the nation. The Duma, the national assembly made up for the most part of representatives chosen by the landowners, was meeting in Petrograd, debating various remedies for Russia's problems. Soviets, councils chosen by working people, were meeting in cities all over the country, discussing particularly the misery caused by Russia's participation in the war against Germany. Much of the blame for the misery was assigned to Alexandra, "the German woman."

The fifteen million men mobilized for the war had left farms untended. Food production dropped. What food there was did not reach the cities because the war put such a strain on the transportation system. Long lines of women were standing outside bakeries waiting to buy bread for their families. On February 24, 1917, the women in Petrograd stopped waiting. They broke into the bakeries and took the bread. That sort of thing had happened before. But this time, when the police were sent to stop the lawlessness, many of the policemen encouraged the women. Workers all over the city left their jobs, and soon the streets were filled with crowds chanting, "Give us bread!" Some shouted, "Down with the war!" and "Down with the German woman!"

WHEN NICHOLAS HEARD THE NEWS HE SENT ORDERS FOR THE army units in the city to disperse the crowds. Some units obeyed, and about two hundred protesters were killed in scattered fighting. But on February 27 about sixty-six thousand soldiers mutinied and joined the crowds. The protesters began to break open prisons and free the prisoners, and to burn government buildings. The protest had become a revolution.

Nicholas's wife was at the Alexander Palace outside the city, giving her full attention to the care of three of their children who had measles. When the cabinet ministers she had appointed saw the soldiers joining the crowds, they gave up any pretense that they could control the situation. That left only one arm of the czar's government functioning in the capital, the Duma. The crowds surrounded the building where the Duma was meeting. Inside, one delegate rose to speak, a brilliant orator named Aleksandr Kerensky. He was one of the few members of the Duma who represented the workers. Kerensky urged that the Duma should now take full responsibility for forming a new government in which workers would be more fairly represented. It would be a temporary, or "provisional," government to serve until a truly representative national assembly could be established. It seemed to the Duma to be worth a try. They chose a cabinet, naming Kerensky as minister of justice. That same day the workers in the city's factories chose delegates to a new council, the Soviet of Workers' and Soldiers' Deputies.

The new cabinet and the new soviet both began issuing proclamations and orders, often at cross-purposes. But cabinet and soviet quickly agreed that a new government had no need for a royal head. Czar Nicholas must abdicate. His generals, left with no troops, advised their sovereign that there was no other course open to him. Later those generals would lead a bitter civil war attempting to reverse the events of the revolution, but just then they could do nothing.

On March 2, 1917, only six days after the women broke into the bakeries, Nicholas did abdicate, ending three centuries of rule by the Romanov dynasty. He wrote in his diary that night that he did it "for the sake of Russia."

Lenin was elected chairman of the new Council of People's Commissars.
Library of Congress

Nicholas rejoined his family at the Alexander Palace. Kerensky and his provisional government thought the family were not safe there from the anger of the people, and tried to arrange for them to go to live in England. When that plan fell through, the government sent them on a special train to the town of Tobolsk in western Siberia. It was a small, old-fashioned town, so far unaffected by revolutionary ideas. Meanwhile the situation in the capital and the country was changing week by week.

The end of the monarchy had been brought about without the direct participation of V. I. Lenin and the other Marxist leaders who had been working for that goal for years. One of the newspapers they published was called the *Spark,* symbol of the beginning of the great fire of revolution. But the spark had been struck in Petrograd by ordinary people acting in desperation. Many of the so-called expert revolutionaries were in exile in Siberia.

Lenin was in Switzerland in 1917, working for the international spread of communism. Ever since the revolution of 1905 had been crushed he had spent more time outside Russia than in, attending meetings of Marxists in various countries and writing eloquent appeals for the overthrow of capitalist governments. He had returned to his native land only occasionally to consult with the Bolshevik branch of the Social Democratic Labor party.

When Russia declared war on Germany in 1914 Lenin saw it as an opportunity for the revolutionaries. Defeat of the Russian armies would lessen the czar's ability to crush a revolution and, equally important, would discredit the czar in the eyes of the people. Germany's leaders saw that revolutionary activities inside Russia would weaken support for the Russian armies, so they began to supply money to Lenin and his followers; and Lenin promised the Germans that if he got control of the government, he would take Russia out of the war. Lenin said he was working for the long-range good of the Russian people. His foes said collaboration with the German enemy made him a traitor. It was a charge that the revolutionaries could never completely escape.

When the revolutionary leaders in exile in Siberia heard that Czar Nicholas had abdicated, they returned to the capital. Lenin also returned, arriving in April 1917. A crowd met him at the train station and bore him on their shoulders into the waiting room formerly reserved for members of the royal family. There he made a speech, proposing that the Bolshevik branch of the Social Democratic Labor party take control of the provisional government set up by Kerensky. The new government would withdraw from the war. Then it would run the nation according to communist principles.

With the provisional government only a month old, even the Bolsheviks were not ready to go as far as Lenin proposed. Kerensky was advocating more gradual reform, in keeping with more moderate socialist principles. Debate continued in the meetings of the cabinet and of the Soviet of Workers' and Soldiers' Deputies.

Meanwhile more and more people's councils—soviets—were being formed all across the nation, to replace the czar's bureaucracy in local governments, even to replace the imperial officer corps in army regiments and naval units. In the cities, workers were taking control of factories. In the countryside, peasants were burning the houses of the landowners and taking possession of the land. In the regions of the czar's empire that had once been independent nations, such as Poland, Finland, and Georgia, patriots talked about a return to independence. Old Russia was crumbling. As news of all these widely scattered developments poured into the capital, the provisional government seemed unable to give shape to a new Russia.

Lenin took his case to the people, speaking at public meetings, writing pamphlets, coining slogans, organizing support for communism. One of his slogans was Bread, Peace, Land. Another was All Power to the Soviets. The key soviet, of course, was the one that Lenin hoped to control, the Soviet of Workers' and Soldiers' Deputies in Petrograd.

Many ordinary Russians liked what Lenin said. Most important, a number of army units simply refused to fight any longer against the Germans. Before the abdication, the czar's government had promised a Russian summer offensive in the east to relieve German pressure on the British and French in France. The provisional government attempted to honor this commitment. But in June 1917, when the command was given to attack, many soldiers sat still in their trenches. A strong counter-attack by the Germans led to a Russian retreat, and it seemed Petrograd itself was in danger.

In July soldiers and sailors in Petrograd marched to the building where the government was meeting and called for the leaders of the Petrograd soviet to take complete control of the government. The soldiers and sailors were joined by half a million citizens. Once again the people had taken action without the direction of the expert revolutionaries.

Lenin and the Bolsheviks felt the action of the soldiers and sailors was premature but quickly joined them. Lenin's participation gave the government grounds to charge that the march was German inspired, and the action failed to win control of the government for the Petrograd soviet. Several Bolshevik leaders were arrested, and Lenin escaped to Finland to plan what to do next. The one man who gained from the action was Aleksandr Kerensky, who was now given the title prime minister. As a step toward the goal of creating a truly representative parliament he directed the soviets all around the nation to send delegates to Petrograd for an All-Russian Congress of Soviets.

Though Lenin's Bolsheviks were a branch of the Social Democratic Labor party, they thought socialist reforms too tame and democratic processes too slow to accomplish what was needed in Russia. The Bolsheviks' goal now was to gather enough strength to insure that a second attempt to take over the government by force would succeed. Lenin's chief helper in marshaling strength was a man who had taken part in the unsuccessful revolution of 1905, the effort that Lenin later called the necessary "rehearsal" for the revolution. That man was a good military strategist and persuasive speaker named Leon Trotsky.

By September 1917 the Bolsheviks had enough support in the Petrograd soviet to elect Trotsky its chairman. By mid-October Trotsky had enough of the soldiers and sailors in Petrograd pledged to the Bolsheviks to insure a successful takeover. Lenin returned from Finland. The All-Russian Congress of Soviets was to meet for a second time on October 25. Lenin set October 24 as the date for the Bolsheviks to act. "October twenty-third would be too soon, October twenty-fifth too late," he said.

These events had a double fascination for the world. Russia was supplying the largest army fighting in the world war. And working people everywhere saw that the theories of Marxism might soon be put into practice. An American writer particularly interested in the problems of the workers was John Reed, born in Portland, Oregon, and graduated from Harvard in 1910. He arrived in Petrograd in September 1917 and immersed himself in the history being made there. His vivid account of what he saw was published in book form as *Ten Days That Shook the World*. Lenin called it "a truthful and most vivid exposition of the events" and enlisted Reed's skill with words in the cause of the revolution. Later the Soviet film director Sergey Eisenstein made his own version of those events, using the same title. And later still, the American actor Warren Beatty made a film about John Reed, titled *Reds*.

OVERLEAF:
Lenin speaks to a crowd in Saint Petersburg about the plans of his Bolshevik party for a new Communist government for Russia.
National Council of American Soviet Friendship, Inc.

The ten days that had such profound effects were marked by great excitement, crowds filling the streets, rumors, posters, proclamations, but surprisingly little violence. The great shedding of blood was to come later. On the night Lenin had chosen, October 24, armed Bolsheviks occupied the railroad stations, telegraph offices, post offices, and other public buildings in Petrograd. Kerensky escaped from the city and tried unsuccessfully to find some troops to help him resist. The next afternoon the Bolsheviks surrounded the Winter Palace, where cabinet ministers of the provisional government were meeting. The sailors on the cruiser *Aurora*, taking the Bolshevik side, fired some harmless shots from their cannons. The few guards who were responsible for protecting the palace soon disappeared. At two o'clock on the morning of October 26 the cabinet ministers were arrested.

Later on October 26 the All-Russian Congress of Soviets set up a new government, the Council of People's Commissars. The chairman of the new council was V. I. Lenin. The commissar for foreign affairs was Leon Trotsky. The council member put in charge of nationality affairs was an expert revolutionary from Georgia, south of the Caucasus Mountains, who had taken the name Joseph Stalin.

The council issued two decrees intended to make Lenin's slogan—Bread, Peace, Land—a reality. The first called for immediate negotiations among all the warring nations in Europe to end their war. The second abolished private ownership of large estates, putting the land of the nobles and of the church under the control of "peasants' soviets."

Lenin's measures still seemed too extreme to many socialists. In hopes of regaining a voice in the government, they formed in Petrograd the Committee for the Salvation of the Country and of the Revolution. In Moscow the Bolsheviks had to fight for a week to gain control of the city. In other cities around the nation the Bolsheviks had varying success. Patriots in the Ukraine and Finland proclaimed independence from Russia. But Lenin controlled the capital and most of the armed forces, so his was the dominant voice in setting the course of the next few months.

The idea of a truly representative parliament had been talked about for a hundred years, since the days of Czar Alexander I. Kerensky's provisional government had set elections for mid-November. Although Lenin scorned "bourgeois parliaments," he saw that it would be unwise to cancel these elections. The Bolsheviks won only 25 percent of the seats. But that did not matter. Marx taught that a successful revolution must be followed by a period of dictatorship in order to accomplish the drastic changes needed to establish a Communist state. Lenin was the dictator for Russia. When the delegates elected to the parliament met in January 1918 and rejected Lenin's plan to give all power to the soviets, the Bolshevik delegates simply walked out. Then two hundred soldiers and sailors loyal to Lenin forced the delegates to adjourn. The next day Lenin dissolved the parliament. That was the same ploy Czar Nicholas had used when he did not like the actions of the Duma. It was clear all power had in fact gone to the soviets.

To protect that power, Lenin reestablished the secret police force that the czars had used to root out any form of subversive activities. It is said that some members who not long ago were spying on Marxist organizers changed over willingly to spying on those who opposed Marxism.

RUSSIA'S ENEMIES, GERMANY AND AUSTRIA, WERE GLAD TO begin peace negotiations with Lenin's government, and sent delegations to a peace conference in the town of Brest Litovsk in Poland. Russia's allies, France and Great Britain, did not send delegations because they had an agreement with the czar's government that none of the Allies would make a separate peace in the war. The German delegation demanded that Germany be allowed to keep the territory then occupied by her troops, which included much of Poland. Lenin believed that the Marxist revolution would soon spread to Germany and that the main objective of the peace conference was to stop Russian losses in the war. Therefore he agreed to the German demand. The peace treaty of Brest Litovsk was signed in March 1918. The Germans and Austrians were then able to concentrate their forces against the British and French on the western front. But the withdrawal of Russia from the war was more than offset by the addition of the United States to the Allied side. The U.S. Congress had declared war on Germany on April 6, 1917, and American men, tanks, and airplanes helped win numerous battles. On November 11, 1918, the Germans asked for an armistice, and the world war was over. Diplomats from thirty-two nations met at the Palace of Versailles near Paris to decide terms of peace.

Russia's leaving the war eight months earlier did not produce all the benefits Lenin hoped for. The Russian armies came back from the front, but the revolution's debates held little interest for the ordinary soldiers, who wanted only to head for their homes to protect their families. Perhaps they could get a share of the large estates that had been handed over to the local soviets.

On the other hand, some of the military officers were still loyal to the czar and began to organize a counterrevolution to reverse Lenin's work altogether. Other officers supported the moderate socialist objectives of the Committee for the Salvation of the Country and of the Revolution as alternatives to Lenin's ideas.

Lenin knew his victories in the first weeks of the revolution would be challenged militarily. He gave his commissar for foreign affairs, Leon Trotsky, a new title, commissar for war. Trotsky organized an army and named it the Red Army, for the color of the banner of international Marxism. The Russians who fought against the Reds called themselves the White armies. By mid-1918 a disastrous civil war was in progress. Because the Bolsheviks were strongest in Petrograd, the White armies went into action far from the capital, in areas where they hoped to win local support. One such area was the basin of the Don River, where the cossacks had a tradition of independence from the government in the capital. Other areas were the once-independent Ukraine, Georgia, Poland, and the Baltic states of Estonia, Latvia, and Lithuania. The White armies did gather some support for a fight against the Bolsheviks, but each general led his own army and they couldn't agree on the type of government to be established in place of Lenin's dictatorship. That made unified action impossible.

Some of the White army leaders wanted to restore the Romanov dynasty, or at the very least insure the safety of Czar Nicholas and his family by escorting them out of Russia. But the new government saw danger in a royal family that could serve as a rallying point for opposition, and in July 1918 Nicholas, Alexandra, and their five children were taken from Tobolsk to the Bolshevik-dominated town of Ekaterinburg nearby. There they were shot—in secret so that no one would be held responsible. Rumors continued for years that one or more of them had escaped, particularly the youngest daughter, Anastasia. But the executioners were very thorough.

In 1918, before the world war ended, fourteen foreign countries sent troops into Russia to aid the White armies, in hopes the Russians would

Тов. Ленин ОЧИЩАЕТ
землю от нечисти.

This 1920 poster reads "Lenin Cleans the World." It shows him sweeping away monarchs, priests, and capitalists.

continue to fight the Germans. One of those countries was the United States. A young British statesman, Winston Churchill, had persuaded President Woodrow Wilson that the Communist revolution was a threat to all capitalist countries. A joint British, French, and American Expeditionary Force landed at Arkhangel'sk on Russia's north coast. Other American forces landed at Vladivostok on the Pacific coast.

85

Even with outside help, the White armies were no match for the Reds. Their efforts were scattered geographically, and they lacked a unified command and program. The Reds controlled the transportation system of the country, and Lenin and Trotsky gave their soldiers clear goals and effective strategy. By 1920 it was clear the White cause was hopeless. The soldiers were exhausted. The counterrevolution was over.

Many of the czar's officers left Russia. Numbers of dispossessed landowners had already fled, taking with them what wealth in gold and jewels they could conceal in the hems and linings of their clothing. Many had business and family connections abroad. Russian communities grew up in many of the world's major cities. Paris and Shanghai were particularly favored refuges. Sergey Diaghilev, a genius of Russian ballet, assembled a troupe that toured the world for many years as the Ballet Russe de Monte Carlo. There is still a Russian Society in New York City, where imperial titles of nobility continue in use and traditional Russian holidays are observed with splendid balls.

THE AMERICAN EXPEDITIONARY FORCE SENT TO ARKHANGEL'SK returned home in late 1919, having accomplished nothing except to leave the memory in Russian minds that the United States once invaded Russia. All the nations that had intervened to assist the counterrevolution were tired of fighting. It was time for the diplomats to sort out the gains and losses from the world war and to seek what idealists called "a just and lasting peace." To balance all the conflicting claims, the map of Europe would have to be redrawn.

Russia had sent the most troops to the world war. Two and a half million of them were killed or wounded. The civil war had cost the lives of another twenty million Russian soldiers and civilians, dead from injuries, disease, or starvation. The new Russia was off to a terrible start. To make matters worse, droughts in 1920 and 1921 ruined the wheat crop and caused a famine all over the country. That brought the Americans back, this time bringing food and medical supplies. The relief effort was directed by an American engineer, Herbert Hoover, who was elected president of the United States seven years later.

The Bolsheviks were now the undoubted rulers of Russia, but the hardships the people were enduring led to all sorts of protests. The farmers wanted the land that had been taken from the nobles and

In 1921, a year after Lenin won control of Russia, scenes like this were common as a terrible famine afflicted the nation.
Library of Congress

the church to be given to the families who worked on it. They rejected the Communist idea of land owned by the state for the benefit of all. The farmers refused to supply food to the cities or to serve in the Red Army. In Petrograd workers went on strike against factories supposedly owned by "the workers' state." At the nearby Kronstadt naval base the sailors and civilian workers held a mass meeting and adopted a resolution expressing their disappointment with the Bolsheviks they had helped put in power.

The Bolsheviks reacted to all these protests with military force. Thirteen sailors at Kronstadt were executed at once, and many more later. Teams organized by Joseph Stalin used their guns to compel the farmers to hand over food. But it was obvious that the workers' paradise the Marxists had promised had definitely not arrived in Russia. Men and women would not always work for the common good of all. When they were hungry, they wanted their work to produce food for the table in a plain, direct way.

The new Communist government boasted that Soviet women joined gladly with men in building communism, including working on the railroads.
Library of Congress

In 1921 Lenin announced his New Economic Policy. This policy permitted more private enterprise than strict Communist theory allowed. His practical bending of belief in the face of reality soon produced an economic recovery. Lenin invited foreign capitalists to invest in Russia, and many did so.

The government of the new Russia was the fifteen-member Council of People's Commissars—Lenin, Trotsky, Stalin, and the other Bolshevik leaders—established on the day after the Bolsheviks seized power. That was the reality. But Lenin could not ignore the long quest for a constitution to provide representative government for the nation. So he proposed that the area around Petrograd and Moscow, the area where his control was strongest, be made a republic with a constitution. He called it the Russian Soviet Federated Socialist Republic. The constitution was carefully written so that it provided the forms of representative government but kept the real power in the hands of the Council of People's Commissars. Lenin viewed this republic as the pattern for the organization of the rest of the nation. Other republics would join this one in a national union, the Union of Soviet Socialist Republics. To foster unity he moved his government from Petrograd to the ancient national capital, Moscow.

When the diplomats of the World War I enemies met at Versailles for a peace conference, they recognized the claims to independence of many peoples who had been conquered by the czars: the Finns, Estonians, Latvians, Lithuanians, Poles, Byelorussians, Ukrainians, Moldavians, Georgians, Armenians, and the Azeri living in Azerbaijan. These national groups all set up their own governments, with their own constitutions. But in Byelorussia, Ukraine, Georgia, Armenia, and Azerbaijan, Marxists convinced the governments that they needed protection from being taken over by their neighbors and should join Lenin's union. In December 1922 they became part of the new Union of Soviet Socialist Republics. Within a year Great Britain, France, Italy, and other European countries gave diplomatic recognition to the USSR as a new nation. Over the next twelve years the southern parts of the former empire of the czars were added as republics, with names that acknowledge the ethnic identities of their citizens: Turkmenistan, Uzbekistan, Tadzhikistan, Kazakhstan, Kirgizia. Those ethnic identities are still very strong in people's minds, despite seventy years of exhortation glorifying "Soviet man."

CHAPTER SIX
STALIN —
MAN OF STEEL

ITH THE ESTABLISHMENT OF THE UNION OF SOVIET Socialist Republics in 1922 it might seem that the goal of Lenin's life was achieved. He had a brilliant mind, and as a young man he had mapped out a path to the realization of the Communist society envisioned by Karl Marx. One of Lenin's early books was entitled *What Is to Be Done?* But the Communist revolution had not happened the way he had planned or Marx had predicted. It had not begun in a highly industrialized nation but in Russia, where most of the population lived on farms. It had not been begun by expert professional revolutionaries but by ordinary citizens standing in line to buy bread. It had not served as the spark that would start a wider revolution sweeping across Europe. In fact, in Lenin's own native land the citizens were so slow to accept Marxist goals that he had had to adopt the New Economic Policy, reinstating some capitalist free enterprise incentives, in order to get farm and factory production up to levels adequate to provide for the population.

In 1922 Lenin was fifty-two years old. His constant work for the revolution had exhausted even his great energy. It was time to think about who would carry on his work after him. There were seven other members of the policy-making committee of the Communist party, called the Politburo. His second-in-command ever since the revolution had been Leon Trotsky, who like Lenin had traveled widely in Europe working to spread communism. But as a result of his travels Trotsky was not well known in Petrograd when he joined Lenin there in 1917, and his sharp tongue had made him few friends since. He did not seem a wise choice as Lenin's successor.

Joseph Stalin, the member responsible for nationality affairs, was probably the next most likely choice. He had a genuine right to speak for the workers, since his father worked in a shoe factory and his mother had worked as a laundress and a seamstress to pay for her son's education. He was thoroughly aware that the USSR was made up of many different ethnic groups, since he belonged to one of the most fiercely independent of these groups, the mountaineers of Georgia in the Caucasus. His real name was Iosif (the Russian form of Joseph) Vissarionovich Dzhugashvili—he had taken the name Stalin, meaning Man of Steel, after many arrests for revolutionary activity.

Dzhugashvili was born in 1879 in the village of Gori. Almost the only schools available to a poor Georgian were those offered by the church. When Joseph graduated at age fourteen from the village school, he was awarded a small scholarship to the church seminary in the capital of Georgia, Tiflis (now called Tbilisi). The six-year course there was intended to prepare students to be priests, but the faculty knew many of the boys enrolled with no intention of following that vocation. In fact the ideas for national reform that were sweeping the universities were also actively discussed by the students in the seminary. When he was eighteen Joseph began meeting with other students and workers to discuss workers' rights. He found politics more interesting than religion, and a year before he was due to graduate he did not take a required examination. That lost him his place in the seminary. After that he concentrated on converting men to Marxism, as taught by the Russian Social Democratic Workers party.

For May Day 1901 Joseph helped organize the first Marxist demonstration in Tiflis. In 1902, when he was twenty-two, the party sent him to organize workers' demonstrations at an oil refinery in Azerbaijan. For that work the czar's police arrested him, his first arrest of many. All the Marxists expected to go to jail and viewed a jail sentence as a sort of certification of their value to the cause. After a year in jail Joseph was sentenced to three years of political exile. V. I. Lenin had spent his exile writing a book. But Joseph liked action more than words. He escaped

Joseph Stalin, the Man of Steel, in 1934
Library of Congress

from custody and by 1904 was back in Georgia. The Social Democratic Workers party was now split into Mensheviks and Bolsheviks. Joseph joined the Bolsheviks, the followers of Lenin.

January 9, 1905, was Bloody Sunday, when government troops fired on the workers marching in Saint Petersburg to present a petition to the czar. Resentment of this action was particularly strong in Georgia, where violence continued for months. That year the work of Dzhugashvili came to the attention of Lenin, and the two men met for the first time at a Bolshevik conference in Finland. Government repression and arrests had almost crippled the Bolsheviks, and Lenin was again directing revolutionary activities from outside Russia.

In 1906 Joseph made a speech at a party congress in Stockholm. Between 1908 and 1917 he was arrested and exiled three times. While he was in exile the Central Committee was formed to make the Bolsheviks a separate political party, and Joseph was chosen one of its ten members. In 1912 he managed to meet again with Lenin, who recommended he write a treatise on the relation of Marxism to the question of the many ethnic groups—nationalities—in Russia. He did that, writing that members of every nationality had a right to self-determination and a right to speak their own language and have their own schools. Lenin was pleased and made Joseph responsible for supervising a new newspaper of the Bolsheviks, called *Pravda,* meaning "truth."

In 1913 Joseph's last exile sent him to northern Siberia, where escape was almost impossible; but when Czar Nicholas's government collapsed in 1917, all the political exiles were free to travel. Joseph, now regularly known as Stalin, went at once to Petrograd, arriving several weeks before Lenin returned from Switzerland. In the new government, Lenin recognized Stalin's work by giving him responsibility for nationality affairs in the Council of People's Commissars. He also named him to several important subcommittees.

Stalin was excellent at committee work and at organizing affairs for the new government. Lenin appreciated his directness, compared to the long-winded philosophical arguments of his colleagues.

When the farmers had refused to hand over their grain to the state to feed the people in the cities, Stalin had been Lenin's choice to organize teams to take the grain by force. He had learned a lot about conditions outside the capital. And the tactics he had used to get the grain—informers, hostages, executions—had been quite effective.

Lenin firmly believed the Bolsheviks should do whatever was necessary for the sake of the revolution. This strong-willed Georgian might be the right choice for the next head of state. But if Stalin had more power, how would he use it? In 1922 Lenin created the new position of general secretary of the Central Committee of the Communist party and appointed Stalin to the post.

SHORTLY AFTER STALIN'S APPOINTMENT, LENIN SUFFERED A mild stroke. The question of who would succeed him became more urgent. When he saw that Stalin was maneuvering to acquire even more power for himself, Lenin had second thoughts about the appointment. But before he could undo it, he had two more strokes. On January 21, 1924, Lenin died.

Nadezhda Krupskaya, his widow, published an appeal in the newspaper *Pravda* that there be "no public worship" of the dead leader. Nevertheless, his body was enclosed in a glass coffin and put on display in a specially constructed granite mausoleum in Red Square in Moscow next to the wall of the Kremlin. It is still there, viewed daily by thousands of citizens and foreign tourists. The city Peter the Great had named Saint Petersburg was renamed Leningrad, meaning "Lenin city," a name it kept until 1991. Karl Marx had written, "Religion is the opiate of the people," and these words were carved on monuments and taught to all young Communists. But the substitution of Lenin's name for Saint Peter's, and the pilgrimages to his tomb, suggested to more than one observer that communism was acquiring its own religious shrines and saints.

Old ways die hard. Cities have nicknames, such as L.A. and D.C. in the United States. The nickname of Leningrad continued to be Peter. And the story is told that a young woman taking an examination for a Communist party post was unsure of the answer to a question asking the inscription on a certain monument. She wrote the words of Marx quoted above and when the examination was over hurried to the monument to check. Reading the inscription "Religion is the opiate of the people," she fell to her knees, saying, "Thank God."

•   •   •

LENIN HAD DIED WITHOUT NAMING ANY ONE MAN AS HIS SUC-
cessor. Perhaps he intended the members of the Politburo to work as a
team to direct the nation. But their ideas were too different for that.
Each began seeking the power to back his own ideas. And in the struggle
that followed, the man with the least scruples won the most power.

The strongest contenders were Trotsky and Stalin. Their policy dif-
ferences concerned the future course of communism. Trotsky still believed in working for a worldwide Communist revolution. Stalin believed
it would be more sensible to concentrate efforts in their own country.
Stalin's view had more appeal to the Russian people, fiercely patriotic
but little interested in the affairs of other nations. Stalin won over to his
side two other members of the Politburo and with their help began to
reduce Trotsky's responsibilities and titles. Stalin charged Trotsky with
working against the Communist party, and had him exiled to Siberia
and later banished from the Soviet Union. (Trotsky eventually went to
live in Mexico, where he continued writing his views and even wrote
an uncomplimentary biography of Stalin. He was murdered in Mexico
City in 1940, probably by Stalin's agents.) After Stalin had bested Trotsky
he began to reduce the influence of the two men who had helped him
do so.

In the new Union of Soviet Socialist Republics the Bolsheviks had
set up a power structure that was upside down compared to republics
in other lands. The leaders of the local Communist party organizations
around the country were chosen not by the party members in each town
but by the Central Committee in Moscow. The local leaders then determined who would be admitted to membership in the Communist
party. Stalin used this structure to appoint local leaders who would
support him. He expelled from the party those who opposed him, citing
a resolution, "On Party Unity," passed at the party congress in 1921,
that banned "factional activities." The secret police were still active in
discovering who was criticizing the government, and Stalin declared it
was the duty of every good Communist to expose "disloyalty," even in
the members of one's own family.

In the early years of the Stalin era the New Economic Policy introduced by Lenin in 1921 as a temporary measure continued to have good
results. Industries, helped by investment from abroad, grew. Agricultural
production rose. Stalin saw some farmers were accumulating land and

wealth. These comparatively wealthy farmers he called *kulaks* (meaning "tightfisted"). Some factory owners were also growing rich. But the revolution had been fought to give the nation a Communist system of production, with the benefits Marx promised for all citizens. By 1928 Stalin believed it was time to return to Marxist practice.

He began by announcing a five-year plan for economic development and growth. One basic part of the plan was for factories to be turned over to the government. In theory, government planning would provide more efficient production by eliminating uncertainties of supply and demand. Beyond that, the government could convert factories to produce goods that would contribute to national strength, such as rails for new railroads and large electrical generators for new power plants. Many nations were building dams to generate electricity, and some of the largest in the world were built in the Soviet Union. National strength was a goal the people approved, but Stalin's emphasis on this so-called heavy industry meant fewer factories to produce goods for individuals, such as sewing machines and automobiles.

The second basic part of Stalin's five-year plan was to put all farmland under government control. Small farms owned and worked by individual families would be replaced by huge farms owned by the state. Some would be "state farms," managed like factories by government officials and cultivated by workers who would be paid wages. Most would be "collective farms." For these, Stalin proposed that landowners pool their land, livestock, capital, and labor to form farmers' cooperatives, to be managed democratically by the members, guided by government experts. For both collectives and state farms, government experts would decide what crops would be planted and when. All but a small fraction of the food produced would go into a common stockpile, and other experts would distribute it to all the people of the nation. A tiny fraction of land would be left as "private plots," where families could raise food for their own tables.

Anyone who has seen a skillful farmer coax choice vegetables from a well-loved plot of earth, or who has watched him display them proudly in the local market, will understand that the idea of government-owned farms was not well received. The farmers had a direct way to show their opinion. Many—especially the prosperous kulaks—simply refused to do what Stalin asked.

Stalin was not surprised. He had dealt with the farmers who withheld their grain from the government in the years just after the revolution. Once again he used brutal force. He announced a policy of "eliminating the kulaks as a class." Police and army units surrounded villages and forced the villagers to join the collectives. But many chose to kill their animals and burn their tools and crops rather than have them become property of the state. More than half the farm animals in the nation died as a result. Stalin's punishment for such destruction was confiscation of land, exile to labor camps in Siberia, or death. Thousands of farmers were executed, and millions were sent to Siberia. The state-owned farms could do without their labor, Stalin reasoned. The agricultural experts were modernizing farming. The introduction of tractors and chemical fertilizers would greatly increase the yield of one man's work.

In a few years the results of collectivization of agriculture would be enormous suffering not only for farmers but for the whole nation. But at first the five-year plan seemed to be working. In December 1932 Stalin

A government propaganda photograph posed to show the happy conditions on Soviet collective farms. Reality was much grimmer.
National Council of American Soviet Friendship, Inc.

announced that its goals had been met, nine months ahead of schedule. The Second Five-Year Plan would begin in January 1933. Visitors from other nations came to see for themselves the results of the first large-scale attempt to put into practice the theories of Karl Marx. Communist parties in other countries now looked to the Soviet Union for guidance. The Communist International, an organization founded by Lenin to spread world revolution, was modified by Stalin into a sort of Soviet Friendship Association. He instructed Communists in other countries to stop talking about overthrowing governments and to work to develop friendly relations between those countries and the pace-setting Soviet Union.

The neighbor to the east, China, had replaced its imperial government with a republic in 1911. Young Chinese were sent to Moscow to study the Soviet example. Two of them were Chiang Ching-kuo, son of China's military leader, Chiang Kai-shek; and Chou En-lai, who would become premier after China's own Communist revolution. In the United States, a number of men and women concerned about social problems joined the American Communist party. In 1933 the United States began diplomatic relations with the Soviet Union. In 1934 the Soviet Union was admitted to the League of Nations, the organization founded after World War I to try to settle disputes between nations peacefully.

If visitors to the USSR looked only at the production figures and the tractors in the fields, and listened only to the speeches at the endless official banquets, they went home full of phrases like "Communist utopia" and "workers' paradise." One American writer, Lincoln Steffens, was so impressed that he reported, "I have been over into the future, and it works."

Such favorable judgments were premature. In 1933 the wheat harvest was much below that in 1932. The decrease was in part due to bad weather. But it was also due to the fact that in order to meet quotas, the "experts" had taken from the farms much of the wheat intended for seed for the next year's crop. A national famine resulted, and six million to seven million citizens of the workers' paradise starved to death. Even such a zealot as Stalin could not ignore such a disaster.

Stalin had now been the strongest man in the nation for seven years, since he had discredited Trotsky and his other rivals in the Politburo. But the Central Committee of the Communist party still had the power to vote him out of office. Some of the members had worked with Lenin and could claim that they were following Lenin's teaching when they disagreed with Stalin. Stalin devised a plan that would remove the threat to his power posed by these "old Bolsheviks," and at the same time allow him to escape blame for the famine and other failures of his policies. The assassination of one of his closest associates, Sergey Kirov, gave him the incentive and the opportunity to put this plan into action.

Stalin charged that the assassination was the work of a group of men in the government who were still loyal to the exiled Leon Trotsky. These men, Stalin said, had planned to assassinate him also. Furthermore, they had been working undercover for years to wreck the five-year plan. Stalin ordered the Cheka secret police, now renamed the NKVD (and later again renamed the KGB), to identify and arrest all these conspirators and "wreckers." It soon became clear that anyone who opposed Stalin was subject to arrest. That included anyone who protested that an arrested colleague was innocent. Any reluctance to give evidence against a colleague was interpreted as anti-Stalin feeling.

As hundreds of citizens were arrested, fear of arrest spread. Many cowards thought they could demonstrate their loyalty to Stalin by denouncing someone else. The cowards were often arrested soon after the people they had denounced. The agents of the NKVD were not immune either. If an agent made too few arrests, or spent too much time checking the truth of charges against someone, that agent might be arrested for lack of zeal. Stalin's first charges after Kirov's assassination started a chain reaction. This period in his rule came to be known as the Terror. No one could be sure that he was safe from a knock on the door by the NKVD in the middle of the night. Arrests over a five-year period have been estimated by one Soviet author at between four million and five million.

For Stalin it was not enough to arrest and try so many potential opponents. His plan included the use of the arrests to "educate" all the people of the Soviet Union. The lesson he taught was that only Stalin knew what was best for the nation, and therefore only strict loyalty to his ideas would be tolerated. Children and young people who had known no other ruler accepted this lesson. They gladly joined the youth organizations: Pioneers, Young Octobrists (named for the October Revolution of 1917), and Komsomol (Young Communist League).

So many arrests put an impossible strain on the courts. Many of those arrested were questioned, then sentenced without trial. The same

Soviet author estimates that four hundred thousand to five hundred thousand, about 10 percent of those arrested, were either exiled or executed. To give an appearance of legality to the arrests, and to clinch the "education" of the people, Stalin ordered public trials for a selection of the most prominent officials. By a long ordeal of interrogation, threats, and promises, NKVD agents obtained confessions to acts of treason that were never committed. The trials were carefully staged theater—"show trials."

After Stalin had eliminated the threat to his power from the officials who opposed him, he turned his attention to the nation's military men. This was the group that could have overthrown the government, as military men have done in many nations. But the Terror seems to have paralyzed them too, and they submitted to the arrests.

Stalin called what he was doing a "purge," medicine to remove impurities from the body of the nation so it could grow strong. Historians made a more accurate medical comparison, to the eighteenth-century practice of bleeding patients. The theory was that puncturing a vein and letting supposedly impure blood flow out would cause it to be replaced by healthy new blood. Stalin believed that the old Bolsheviks who had opposed him would be replaced by young Communists with correct ideas—that is to say, with Stalinist ideas. And just as the patient, weakened by the bleeding, frequently died, the USSR came close to dying after Stalin destroyed the best brains in the government and military. The nation soon had to face a strong threat from abroad.

In the period after World War I, in a number of nations, new voices were challenging the ideal of a government that was representative of all the people. What was needed to provide national strength and prosperity, these new leaders maintained, was a central government with total power, headed by one man, a dictator. Basic rights of individuals were ignored. People listened to these challenges because of dissatisfaction with the terms of peace treaties and because of economic problems of unemployment and inflation. Such a government with total power is sometimes called totalitarian. Between 1922 and 1939 such governments were established by Benito Mussolini in Italy, Adolf Hitler in Germany, Francisco Franco in Spain, and a group of military men in Japan. They had various goals and used various tactics, but they shared a passionate opposition to communism anywhere in the world.

Stalin had to take seriously their denunciations of his government.

These dictators were quite willing to use force to get what they wanted. If several of them banded together to attack the Soviet Union, he did not yet have the military strength to resist.

In 1931 Japanese troops invaded China's northeast province of Manchuria, for the second time in the twentieth century. China was a huge country, but still a weak one. A Japanese conquest of Manchuria would put Japan's armies on the borders of the Soviet Union. In 1935 Italian troops invaded the nation of Ethiopia in Africa. The League of Nations protested the aggression of Japan and Italy but did nothing to stop it. In 1936 the Japanese, the Italians, and the Germans signed a treaty they called the Anti-Comintern Pact.

In Spain in 1936 General Francisco Franco led a revolt against the nation's five-year-old republican government. Hitler and Mussolini sent German and Italian troops to help Franco, whose political beliefs were close to their own. Stalin sent supplies to help the Spanish republican government survive. He sent no Soviet troops to Spain, but he directed the Comintern to recruit an International Brigade to fight against Franco. Men and women from a number of nations, including the United States, fought in this brigade because they were concerned that the totalitarians were gaining strength in Europe. After nearly three years of civil war Franco won the power struggle. The German and Italian troops, now tested in battle, returned home. Stalin, along with the rest of the world, watched to see what the totalitarian leaders would do next.

CHAPTER SEVEN

ALLIES IN A WORLD WAR

$\mathfrak{J}$N 1939 THE GREATEST THREAT TO THE SOVIET UNION WAS the ambition of the German Nazi leader Adolf Hitler. He had risen to power in 1933 by proclaiming that the German people were a "master race," destined to rule all of Europe. Two groups stood in their way and must be dealt with, he said: the Jews and the Communists. Hitler sent millions of German Jews to concentration camps, where they were forced to labor for the state, and millions were systematically killed.

In the Soviet Union, Stalin had also ordered large numbers of citizens to labor camps and had executed many Jews. That part of Hitler's program he understood. But the Nazi dictator's anticommunism bordered on hysteria. Germany had built up its military forces, ignoring the peace treaty that ended World War I. In 1938 Hitler had sent his troops across the border of his neighbor Austria, where the government accepted his control without a fight. Now in 1939 he added Czechoslovakia to his conquests with equal ease, and closer to the Soviet Union, he occupied a part of the small Baltic nation of Lithuania. It seemed clear he might attack the Soviet Union.

To the surprise of the rest of the world, in 1939 Stalin and Hitler signed a treaty. Their negotiations had been carried on in secret. In late

August they announced some agreements about trade between the two countries, and promises that neither would attack the other. What they did not announce was that they had also agreed to divide up the territory that lay between the German and Soviet borders. Germany was to get the western part of Poland. The Soviet Union was to get the eastern part of Poland plus Estonia and Latvia. Lithuania was later promised to Stalin as well. In addition, Germany agreed that Finland was a natural part of the "sphere of influence" of the Soviet Union.

On September 1, 1939, just a week after the treaty was signed, German troops invaded Poland from the west. Britain and France immediately declared war on Germany but sent no troops to help Poland. And on September 17 Soviet troops invaded Poland from the east. Poland's cause was hopeless. In the following weeks Estonia, Latvia, and Lithuania were also occupied by Soviet troops. In none of these countries was there effective resistance.

In November the Soviets invaded Finland. But there the story was different. The Finns fought doggedly all through the winter until March 1940. Stalin's diplomats explained to the world that the Soviet Union was simply reclaiming territory that had belonged to the nation under the czars and that such action was necessary to protect her borders. Other diplomats were not impressed by these explanations. In December 1939 the League of Nations expelled the Soviet Union from membership. But by then the league had lost any influence it had on world developments.

In the spring of 1940 it became clear why Hitler had signed the treaty with the major Communist power, the Soviet Union. The memory of conducting battles on two fronts during World War I was still vivid in German minds. Hitler had offered Stalin the territory in eastern Europe in exchange for his promise not to interfere with German plans in western Europe. In 1940 German armies invaded Denmark, Norway, Holland, Belgium, and France. By June 1940 all those countries had surrendered.

Only Great Britain, protected by the sea and her strong navy, fought on against the Nazi conquest. But Britain served as a rallying point for fighting men of all the conquered nations, who escaped from their countries to fight with the British or organized underground resistance to the Nazis. The new British prime minister, Winston Churchill, met with U.S. president Franklin D. Roosevelt to ask for help in the fight against Hitler. There were many Americans who felt their country should keep hands off the affairs of Europe. But President Roosevelt did arrange to send ships and supplies.

British resistance was the first setback Hitler had had in his plan for the German master race to dominate Europe. He went ahead with the plan nevertheless. On June 22, 1941, he sent his armies and tanks into the Soviet Union, ignoring the 1939 treaty with Stalin. Stalin, knowing how few promises Hitler kept, had signed the treaty to buy time to build up his army in case Germany attacked. The day before the invasion Hitler wrote to Mussolini, "The partnership with the Soviet Union was . . . often very irksome to me, for in some way or other it seemed to break with my whole origin, my concepts, my former obligations." He was soon to find that while partnership with the Communist Soviet Union was irksome, war with it was much worse.

Hitler's military victories in western Europe were due in large part to a tactic he called *blitzkrieg,* meaning "lightning war." His forces, using tanks and trucks, struck without warning and traveled quickly deep into a target nation. He also made effective use of air power to destroy military objectives and great sections of cities as well. He believed that a summer blitzkrieg across the plains of the Soviet Union could capture Moscow before winter's snows stopped the advance.

At first it seemed Hitler might succeed. The most able Soviet military leaders had been executed by Stalin in the name of Communist party purity. Hitler's air strikes inflicted heavy damage on the Soviet air force, destroying on the first day of the invasion twelve hundred planes, eight hundred of them still on the ground. His armies advancing across Ukraine captured Kiev in September and controlled the wheat fields that are the breadbasket of the Soviet Union. In the north, other armies approached Leningrad (today Saint Petersburg again) in August. By November the armies attacking in the center were near Moscow.

Then the people's ancient loyalty to Mother Russia, older far than czars or commissars, said, "Enough." While Stalin called the troops Soviet soldiers and Communist comrades, they called themselves "patriots," and they fought to defend the land they loved against an invader who wanted to take it away from them. The war we call World War II they call the Great Patriotic War. Stalin recognized the difference. On November 7, 1941, the anniversary of the Russian Revolution, he stood on

German Nazi dictator Adolf Hitler directed the invasion of the Soviet Union, ignoring the advice of his generals.
National Archives

top of Lenin's tomb in Red Square as usual to review the annual parade. But in his anniversary speech he cited not the heroes of communism, but the earlier heroes of Russia's history. Scoffing at comparisons of Hitler to Napoléon, he said Hitler resembled Napoléon as much as a kitten does a lion. Thousands of citizens volunteered to form militias, although they had no military training, and suffered terrible casualties when they fought the Germans. As always, the defenders' allies were the vast distances of the nation and the winter weather.

In mid-November the Germans made a concentrated attempt to take Moscow. But the defenders counterattacked and put fifty German divisions out of action, leaving the invaders too little strength to continue the attack on the city. It was the first time Hitler's armies had been stopped. The psychological effect was tremendous for both sides in the war.

On December 7, 1941, Germany's partner Japan attacked the United States naval base at Pearl Harbor, in Hawaii, and other important bases in the Pacific. That brought the United States into the war, joining the Allies—the name given all the nations fighting Germany, Italy, and Japan—against the Axis powers. American men were drafted into the armed forces and trained for battle. American factories were converted to produce planes and tanks and guns and ammunition. Some of the weapons were sent to the Soviet Union. The American media began to portray the Soviets as "our gallant Allies." Cartoons of Bolsheviks with homemade bombs were replaced with cartoons of a friendly Russian bear with the face of Joseph Stalin.

During the winter the Soviet forces in Moscow and Leningrad held off the Germans. Hitler had been so confident of a quick victory that he had not issued his troops winter clothing. The Germans almost completely surrounded Leningrad, beginning a siege they thought would force it to surrender. But when Lake Ladoga, just east of the city, froze, the Soviets managed to keep open a route for supplies across the ice. Units of hardy Siberian troops arrived, dressed in white winter camouflage uniforms that made them seem like ghostly avengers as they made night attacks across the snowy landscape. In the city, food grew terribly scarce, since the ice road could not provide nearly enough for a city of three million people. Tree bark, leather, and all sorts of plants were boiled to extract any kind of nourishment. Fuel was also lacking, so the citizens lived in their heavy winter coats. Children and old people were sent east from the city to towns the invaders had not reached. Hundreds of thousands of the citizens who stayed as defenders died from the cold and hunger. The siege of Leningrad lasted for nine hundred days, until January 1944, but the city was never captured.

In the spring of 1942 the Germans, halted near Moscow and Leningrad, renewed their advance in the south, hoping to capture the oil fields on the shore of the Caspian Sea. By this time they desperately needed a new supply of gasoline for their planes and tanks. By August they had reached the industrial city of Stalingrad (today called Volgograd) on the banks of the Volga River. At that point Hitler made one of his most costly mistakes. His troops could have continued south past Stalingrad to the oil fields. But the city had great symbolic significance for Hitler. It was named for the arch-Communist Stalin, who had fought there in the civil war. Hitler ordered his generals to take Stalingrad before moving on.

The first attack showed that the city's defenses were strong. Hitler's armies, like those of Napoléon in 1812 and Charles XII of Sweden in 1708, were spread out and far from sources of supplies. His generals asked permission to pull back and gather strength. Hitler refused and ordered another attack. But his blitzkrieg tactics did not work against such a city, where every street, every building had to be won by man-to-man, hand-to-hand fighting. In November 1942 the Soviet armies launched a strong counterattack. Bitter fighting continued through December and January. On January 31, 1943, the commander of the German Sixth Army, his supplies gone and his men exhausted, surrendered. It was Hitler's first great defeat, and the first time in the history of Germany that an entire German army had been captured. Some historians call the Battle of Stalingrad the turning point of World War II in Europe. German casualties at Stalingrad have been estimated at six hundred thousand, and Soviet casualties at four hundred thousand.

In the summer of 1943 the Germans launched another offensive east of Kiev, but the Soviets halted them and then pushed them back to Kiev and beyond. After that the Germans were forced out of the country north, south, and center. On June 6, 1944, Allied troops landed on the beaches of the Normandy Peninsula in France. On the eastern front and

---

OVERLEAF:

Citizens of Leningrad (Saint Petersburg) line up for water in World War II. The Germans besieged the city for nine hundred days, but her people never surrendered.
National Council of American Soviet Friendship, Inc.

the western front, slowly Hitler's armies were pushed back into Germany. The nations they had overrun were liberated, with Soviet troops entering Poland, Romania, Bulgaria, Yugoslavia, Hungary, Austria, Moldavia, Estonia, Lithuania, and Latvia.

In April 1945 American and Soviet troops, advancing into Germany itself from two sides, met at the Elbe River. Five days later Hitler committed suicide. On May 8 what was left of the German government surrendered.

SOON AFTER THE BATTLE OF STALINGRAD, WHEN IT HAD become clear that defeat of Germany was certain, the Allied leaders Churchill of Great Britain, Roosevelt of the United States, and Stalin of the Soviet Union had begun to discuss plans for the future. They had met in November 1943 in the city of Tehran in Iran, just south of the Soviet Union. Stalin had pointed out that Soviet troops had suffered by far the most casualties in the war, and had urged that the other Allies quickly open a western front to hasten the end of the war. Roosevelt and Churchill had promised for the spring of 1944 an invasion and attack across France, which had been occupied by the Nazis since 1940.

The Soviet Union, fully involved in fighting the Germans, had not declared war on Japan after the attack at Pearl Harbor in 1941. At Tehran, Roosevelt and Churchill had asked Stalin to join them in fighting the Japanese. The Allied navies had gained control of the Pacific, but Japanese soldiers held on with fanatical zeal to the islands they had conquered. They never surrendered, following the samurai warrior's motto: Death Before Dishonor. It seemed likely that they would fight even harder to defend the islands of Japan itself. And since 1931 Japan had had a large army of occupation in China's rich northeastern province of Manchuria. Stalin had promised that two or three months after the Germans surrendered he would send troops to Manchuria.

Stalin had been more interested in the future of his European neighbors. He had proposed that the Soviet Union be allowed to keep the eastern part of Poland captured in 1939. Churchill had suggested that this loss of Polish territory be offset by giving the Poles some of the eastern part of Germany. On the map of Europe, this would have had the effect of "moving Poland westward," as he put it. But the borders of Germany after the war would be determined by a peace conference, not by the three men meeting at Tehran.

Roosevelt was particularly concerned that a new international organization be formed to maintain peace in the future. The other two leaders had agreed such a "United Nations Organization" was desirable, though they had some questions about how votes would be allotted to countries large and small.

Stalin met again with Roosevelt and Churchill in February 1945 in the resort city of Yalta on the Black Sea. In the years since 1945, the Yalta Conference has been much discussed, and Churchill and Roosevelt much criticized for yielding too much power in eastern Europe to Stalin. The criticism would be more properly directed at the Tehran meeting, since Yalta confirmed agreements already made at the earlier meeting. But later years showed that no matter what Stalin had promised, he was going to use his army of eleven million men to insure a great expansion of Soviet influence in the postwar world.

In July 1945 the Allied leaders urged the Japanese government to make an unconditional surrender, to spare the many lives that would be lost on both sides in an invasion of the home islands of Japan. They warned that the alternative was "the complete and utter destruction" of Japan. This plea and warning were ignored, and on August 6, 1945, a U.S. plane dropped a newly developed weapon, an atomic bomb, on the Japanese city of Hiroshima. Two days later Stalin kept his promise and declared war on Japan. He sent his troops across the Soviet border into Manchuria. On August 14 Japan quit the war.

As Stalin's troops moved into Manchuria so did the troops of the Chinese Communist party leader Mao Tse-tung and those of the Nationalist party leader Chiang Kai-shek. When Stalin withdrew his troops in March 1946 they left Mao's Communist army firmly in control of the northern part of the province. Mao immediately resumed his effort to wrest control of China from her longtime ruler, Chiang. Diplomats from the United States tried unsuccessfully to persuade the two men to cooperate in setting up a new, democratic government. Chiang asked for U.S. military help, but Congress and the American people were unwilling to get involved in a war that seemed likely to continue for many years.

In February 1945 Stalin met with U.S. president Franklin Roosevelt and British prime minister Winston Churchill at Yalta on the Black Sea.
National Archives

The Chinese people were also weary of war and had lost confidence in Chiang. By 1949 Chiang saw defeat of his armies was inevitable, and moved his government to the Chinese island of Taiwan. In October 1949 Mao established a Communist government on the mainland, the People's Republic of China.

Stalin sent his congratulations to Mao. But Mao remembered that as the Soviet troops had gone home, they had taken with them the machinery from many Manchurian factories. They explained they were taking it as "war compensation." The value of the machinery has been put at close to $2 billion. The Soviets put it to work rebuilding their own industry, heavily damaged by the war. These actions of Stalin in Manchuria were a sample of what the world could expect from him in the postwar era.

CHAPTER EIGHT
FOES IN A
COLD WAR

THE POWER STRUCTURE OF THE WORLD IN 1945 WAS VERY different from that before World War II. The war, especially the bombing raids, had caused great destruction of cities and industries in countries on both sides of the conflict. The newest world power, the United States, protected by two wide oceans, had not been bombed and emerged from the war with the strongest economy of any nation. Three former great powers, Germany, Italy, and Japan, were now conquered states, occupied by Allied troops. The nations that had been their colonies now asked for independence. But so did the colonies of the victors. The era of colonialism was over. More than a hundred small independent nations came into being in the years following the war.

The victorious Allies sought to arrange the affairs of nations in such a way that the needs of all peoples would be met and there would be no further incentives for war. Even before their victory, they had begun to set up the United Nations Organization to try to insure lasting peace. Such an approach was quite different from that of earlier centuries, when the victors often divided up the territory of the vanquished. (Catherine the Great's dividing up of Poland with Prussia and Austria in the eighteenth century was a typical example.) As it turned out, although Joseph

Stalin supported the United Nations Organization with his words, he acted like a conquering monarch.

A basic principle declared by the Allies, Stalin included, was that the people of every nation should have the right to elect the government they wanted. The plan was that the troops that had occupied Germany, Italy, and Japan would stay only long enough to set up elections and see to it that the new governments were stable, and then go home. But Germany had been invaded from two sides, and was occupied in the west by troops of the United States, Britain, and France, and in the east by troops of the Soviet Union. Berlin, the capital, was located in the east but was occupied by troops of all four nations.

It soon became clear that Stalin had no intention of working with the other nations to create a freely elected government for Germany. Only a Communist government would suit him. And if he could not get one for all of Germany, he would at least get one in the part occupied by his troops. And so in May 1949 two governments were established: the German Democratic Republic in the east and the Federal Republic of Germany in the west. The United States, Britain, and France insisted on keeping their troops in Berlin, however, and kept the western half of the city free of Soviet control.

In the other nations that the Soviets had "liberated" from the Nazis, Stalin followed the same course. He kept Latvia, Lithuania, Estonia, and Moldavia as republics of the USSR. Backed by his troops, Communists won control of the governments in Poland, Czechoslovakia, Hungary, Romania, and Bulgaria. Stalin cut off contact between those nations and the nations of Western Europe. Winston Churchill declared that "an iron curtain" had now descended across the middle of Europe. Behind that curtain, five nations had become "satellites" of the Soviet Union.

In many other nations, including the new ones formed after the war, men and women who accepted the teachings of Karl Marx were campaigning against what they saw as the ills of capitalism. Stalin gave them support in money and advisers. In Italy and in France, Communist candidates won a number of seats in the national legislatures.

Stalin's agents were particularly active in Greece and Turkey. Many powerful Americans were concerned that these two nations might be invaded by the USSR. In March 1947 President Harry S. Truman proclaimed the Truman Doctrine: The United States would help any nation

*American C-54 transport planes unloading food at Tempelhof Airport in the Berlin
Airlift of 1948, which thwarted a Soviet blockade*
National Archives

resist an attack by Communist armies. As a precaution the United States
sent military aid to Greece and Turkey. No invasion occurred.

Belief in capitalism was still strong in the United States. The secretary
of state, George C. Marshall, saw that the sooner the economies of the
nations of Western Europe recovered from the destruction of the war,
the better it would be for the economies of all nations. He proposed
that the United States give financial aid on an unprecedented scale for
rebuilding, and give it not only to the nations that had fought on the

Allied side, but to Germany and Italy as well. Marshall's vision of the future was quite accurate, and the Marshall Plan did in time produce unprecedented prosperity. But his proposal was not immediately accepted by the U.S. Congress.

Some congressmen were reluctant to spend more money outside the United States after the enormous cost of the war. Others had returned to the traditional reluctance to get involved in the affairs of other nations. But many were alarmed by the number of Communists elected to office in European nations. So the Marshall Plan was voted through Congress, in part for the positive objective of creating a healthy world economy and in part for the negative objective of opposing communism. Aid began to flow in 1948.

Understandably Stalin viewed the Marshall Plan as directed against the Soviet Union. In East Germany, troops of Britain, France, the United States, and the Soviet Union were still stationed in Berlin. In 1948 Stalin closed the highways and railroads to the city to prevent the supplies of the other three nations from getting in. Instead of removing their troops, those nations assembled a fleet of planes to form an "air bridge" to the city. In the busiest hours of the Berlin Airlift one plane landed every forty-five seconds. Each day eight thousand tons of supplies were flown in. After almost a year Stalin finally lifted the blockade.

The success of the Berlin Airlift demonstrated that firm action could influence Stalin where words and protests could not. To insure a united response to whatever he did in the future, in 1949 nine nations of Western Europe, plus Great Britain, Canada, and the United States, formed the North Atlantic Treaty Organization (NATO). The NATO treaty allowed the United States to maintain military bases in all of the participating countries. In 1955 the Soviet Union responded with its own Warsaw Mutual Defense Pact, which formalized the existing military situation in the satellite countries.

The United States and the Soviet Union were now by far the strongest nations in the world. Journalists coined a term for them—"the superpowers"—and said they were engaged in a "cold war," a contest for power that stopped short of military aggression. The cold war continued for many years.

•　　•　　•

ON THE OPPOSITE SIDE OF THE SOVIET UNION, IN ASIA, WAR had never really stopped. The Allies had defeated Japan, and Japanese armies had withdrawn from China and Korea. But the Chinese Communist party leader Mao Tse-tung had established a Communist government on the mainland, the People's Republic of China. U.S. congressmen made angry speeches about who was to blame for "the loss of China." In both Moscow and Washington observers asked which Asian nation would be the next to join the Communist side.

Attention soon focused on China's neighbor, Korea, located on a peninsula jutting out from the mainland of Asia. Korea had been conquered by Japan in 1910 and had been guaranteed independence by the Japanese terms of surrender at the end of World War II. When the Japanese armies withdrew from Korea, the northern half of the nation—down to the thirty-eighth parallel of latitude—was occupied by Soviet troops, and the southern half of Korea was occupied by troops of the other Allied nations. The troops in the south supervised election of a government made up of several parties. The Soviets in the north supervised election of a government run by the Communist party. The governments both north and south claimed to represent the entire nation. In June 1950 the Communist government in the north, backed by Stalin and Mao, sent troops across the thirty-eighth parallel, with the announced objective of reunifying Korea. The cold war had become a hot war.

The invasion was the first major test of the effectiveness of the new United Nations Organization. Representatives of all the member nations met once a year for sessions of the General Assembly. When the General Assembly was not meeting, important business was considered by the Security Council, made up of five permanent members—representing the United States, the Soviet Union, Great Britain, France, and China—and five members elected for two-year terms, representing other nations. Any of the five permanent members of the Security Council has the right to veto any action taken. The Soviet delegate had halted many actions in this way. But when the council met to consider the aggression in Korea, the Soviet delegate was absent. So there was no Soviet veto when the Security Council condemned the invasion and recommended that all member nations send aid to South Korea. The United States moved troops there from Japan. Fifteen other nations sent troops, and forty-one sent supplies for the United Nations peacekeeping force, under the command of U.S. general Douglas MacArthur. By November the United Nations force had driven north all the way to Korea's border with China.

The Chinese Communists sent troops to assist the North Koreans. Stalin sent supplies but was not willing to have his troops fight against troops of the United States. In 1949 the Soviet Union had successfully tested an atomic bomb, but neither Stalin nor U.S. president Truman was willing to use this terrible weapon in Korea.

The North Koreans, aided by the Chinese, pushed the United Nations force back south across the thirty-eighth parallel. After seesaw fighting, both sides dug in along a line just north of the parallel.

On June 23, 1951, the Soviet delegate to the United Nations proposed a cease-fire in the war. Representatives of both sides met for two years to discuss peace terms, while reduced fighting continued. It seems likely that the chief obstacle to a final agreement was Joseph Stalin, who was quite content to have both the United States and China drained of men and money by war in Korea.

On March 5, 1953, Stalin died. After that progress at the peace talks was rapid, and a truce was signed July 27, 1953.

JOSEPH STALIN HAD BEEN DICTATOR OF THE SOVIET UNION FOR thirty years. Like Lenin, he had made no definite plans for a successor. A struggle for power in the Communist party naturally followed his death. That struggle was won by a fifty-nine-year-old Politburo veteran, Nikita Khrushchev, who was named First Secretary of the Central Committee of the Communist party in September 1953. As in the case of Lenin and Stalin, the man who held this top post in the party was the most powerful man in the Soviet Union. Later Khrushchev won the added title of chairman of the Council of Ministers.

Nikita Khrushchev was born in 1894, in southwest Russia, the son of a coal miner. When he was fifteen he went to work in the mines, repairing machinery. In 1918 he joined the Red Army to fight for the success of Lenin's revolution and after that devoted his enormous energy to the Communist cause. He studied management at a Communist party school, and by 1938 he had worked his way up to the post of First Secretary of the Communist party of Ukraine and a seat in the Politburo. In the war against Hitler he took part in the defense of Stalingrad and after the war won a post in the party's Central Committee. As a result of his earlier experience in Ukraine, the breadbasket of the Soviet Union, his major interest was agricultural policy.

Khrushchev used tricks and deceit to get the top job just as Stalin had after the death of Lenin. But it soon became apparent how different from Stalin the new leader was. Stalin spent most of his last years inside the Kremlin or at his country villa, seeing only those closest to him, brooding about plots against him, growling orders, making occasional public appearances on Communist holidays. Khrushchev seemed to be everywhere, and he rarely stopped talking.

Khrushchev wanted all Soviet citizens to eat better, and he had two plans to increase Soviet production of food. One was to improve Stalin's collective farm system by combining the hundreds of thousands of collectives into larger, more efficient units and by paying the workers in cash rather than in a portion of the crop. His other plan was to send workers to plant crops in the vast, untouched lands east of the Ural Mountains. He traveled around the nation explaining these plans, getting acquainted with people, and urging them to work hard to make the plans succeed. When people asked him for more production of things like washing machines and automobiles, he promised to take care of that later, since, like Lenin and Stalin before him, he put steel mills and power plants for the nation ahead of goods for individuals. He reduced the number of young men drafted into the army.

After Khrushchev felt his power was secure he announced that the Twentieth Communist Party Congress would be held in February 1956. At a secret session—one from which all foreigners and the news media were banned—he made a long speech, forty-three pages of fine print. In it he denounced his predecessor Stalin and detailed some twenty-five charges against him ranging from his purges and repressions to his failure to deal more effectively with Adolf Hitler. He asked the delegates to keep discussion of these charges within the party, but four months later the U.S. Department of State published the full text of Khrushchev's speech. In time many monuments to Stalin were taken down, his body was removed from its place of honor beside Lenin in Red Square, and the city of Stalingrad was renamed Volgograd. Those victims of Stalin's political repressions who were still alive were released from the labor camps.

Once Khrushchev, the head of state, had criticized Stalin and his works, other citizens spoke out too. Writers led the way. Boris Pasternak wrote a powerful novel, *Doctor Zhivago*, that showed the ills of the country through an account of one man's long life. Government censors would not allow the novel to be published in the Soviet Union, but it was read in other countries around the world and made into a popular motion picture in the mid-1960s. Pasternak was awarded the Nobel Prize for literature in 1958. In 1962 another work, even more revealing of conditions under Stalin, was published in the Soviet Union: *One Day in the Life of Ivan Denisovich* by Aleksandr Solzhenitsyn. This account of life in the labor camps was followed by the same author's *Gulag Archipelago*. Both were widely read in the West. The poet Yevgeny Yevtushenko toured the world giving readings of his poems. He attracted large audiences by the force of his words and the attractiveness of his personality. Filmgoers also learned about the Soviet Union through such award-winning films as *The Cranes Are Flying* and *Ballad of a Soldier*.

Music lovers were already familiar with such contemporary composers as Sergey Prokofiev, Dmitry Shostakovich, and Aram Khachaturian. Prokofiev's *Peter and the Wolf* competes for children's favor with Tchaikovsky's *Nutcracker Suite* from the last century. Khachaturian's "Saber Dance" from his ballet *Gayne* led the classical hit parade for a while. While these composers' works were being performed regularly in the West, the commissars at home occasionally baffled audiences by banning their music for "capitalist," or "anti-Communist," tendencies.

Khrushchev allowed two capitalist institutions, the Boston Symphony Orchestra and the London Philharmonic, to visit Moscow and Leningrad. And he allowed the Soviet violinist David Oistrakh to go on concert tours. Even more rashly, he sent the Bolshoi Ballet Company, perhaps the world's greatest, on tour. In time ballet dancers would have a political significance Khrushchev never expected.

The actions of the new Soviet leader were naturally of great interest to policymakers in the United States. They soon produced a thaw in the cold war. Khrushchev met with U.S. president Dwight Eisenhower in July 1955 in Geneva, Switzerland. At Geneva both Khrushchev and Eisenhower renounced the use of atomic bombs—though both nations continued to develop and test ever more powerful versions of such weapons. In February 1956 Khrushchev called for "peaceful coexistence" of the superpowers. Because he was convinced that communism was superior to capitalism, he expected future victories without war: The Soviet Union would grow stronger, and capitalist nations would perish because of "internal contradictions of capitalism." It was this view that communism would outlive capitalism that led him to say to capitalists, "We will bury you"—that is to say, we will be alive to come to your funeral. The words have been often misinterpreted as a threat of victory through violence.

Peaceful coexistence did not mean that the Soviet Union would shirk what it saw as its obligation to persuade developing nations to choose the Communist path—nor did Khrushchev expect the United States to cease its efforts to expand the number of nations in its camp. Power was the goal of each superpower. Expansion was the means. "Peaceful coexistence" was a pleasant-sounding pair of words to be used by speech writers.

THE CHANGE IN COMMAND IN MOSCOW MADE PEOPLE IN SOME of the satellite countries hope for a loosening of Soviet control over their affairs. Strikes and revolts occurred in Poland and Hungary. But the thaw in the cold war was only partial. While Khrushchev allowed a bit more influence to national leaders, he kept troops in place to insure that none of the satellites broke away completely.

In Poland two men had been arrested in Stalin's last years for advocating more independence from the Soviet Union. One was the head of the Roman Catholic church in Poland, Stefan Cardinal Wyszyński. The other was a labor leader, Wladyslaw Gomulka. In the summer of 1956 strikes and riots in several Polish cities caused Khrushchev to relax Moscow's control a bit, which allowed the reinstatement of Cardinal Wyszyński and the election of Gomulka as First Secretary of the Polish Communist party. Thirty years later cooperation between the church and the labor unions would make Poland the first Soviet satellite to succeed in breaking free.

In Hungary the leader of the drive to reduce Soviet influence was Imre Nagy. He was elected premier in 1956 and promptly proclaimed that Hungary was neutral in the contest between East and West. To demand withdrawal of all Soviet troops from their country, thousands of Hungarian freedom fighters filled the streets in the capital, Budapest.

Russian tanks ended the Hungarian drive to become free of Soviet influence.
Embassy of Hungary

The women of the city urged them on, shouting from their windows, "Go, boys, go!" Street fighting went on for several days before Soviet tanks put an end to it. Two thousand nine hundred Hungarians died, thirteen thousand were wounded, and two hundred thousand left their homeland to seek freedom in many countries of the world. Khrushchev put in his own man to replace Nagy, who was executed. These events indicated that coexistence might be possible with another superpower of equal strength, but those without equal tanks could expect different treatment.

CHAPTER NINE
VICTORIES IN SPACE, STAGNATION ON EARTH

$\mathcal{A}$S THE 1950S DREW TO A CLOSE, EAST GERMANY WAS STILL firmly under Soviet control. West Germany was going its own way, with an independent government receiving help but not orders from the West. It was clear to everyone which Germany had a stronger economy and higher standard of living. But neither Germany had signed a peace treaty with the victors in World War II—the United States, Britain, France, and the Soviet Union. The Soviet head of state, Nikita Khrushchev, said it was time to sign such treaties and to remove the Western troops still in West Berlin and West Germany. To discuss that, the foreign ministers of the four victors met in May 1959. Another thaw in the cold war seemed possible.

In July 1959 U.S. vice president Richard Nixon visited the Soviet Union. In Moscow he opened an exhibition intended to introduce to Soviet citizens American arts and commercial goods, including household appliances. Khrushchev visited the exhibition and began a conversation with Nixon about a device to squeeze lemons that was on display. Both were men of strong convictions, and the conversation soon developed into a lively discussion of the merits of two political systems. Journalists were delighted to report what they called the Kitchen Debate.

In September 1959 Khrushchev visited the United States and toured

*In 1959 Richard M. Nixon, then U.S. vice president, joined Soviet head of state
Nikita Khrushchev in opening a trade fair in Moscow.*
National Archives

the country in President Eisenhower's official airplane. The Soviet leader's
bubbling energy and genuine enthusiasm earned him a generally warm
welcome, especially when he asked to change his itinerary to include a
visit to Disneyland in California. But, he wrote in his memoirs, "some
people had decided to stage an organized demonstration against me. . . . I
decided not to insist." He visited a large farm in Iowa, owned by Roswell
Garst, a man who had had great success growing hybrid corn and who
had met with Khrushchev in the Soviet Union. "Garst . . . was the sort
of man you could profitably listen to," Khrushchev later wrote. "To tell
the truth, he usually did all the talking while I just listened. He knew
agriculture backwards and forwards." If that is the truth, Garst was one
of the few men in the world who could outtalk Khrushchev.

The Soviet leader received a visit from Nelson Rockefeller, then governor of the state of New York, whom he remembered as "not just a plain capitalist, but the biggest capitalist in the world." Khrushchev invited Eisenhower's grandchildren to visit the Soviet Union, advising them not to come during a Russian winter. Some Americans began to wonder about their grim stereotypes of Soviet Communists.

At the end of his stay Khrushchev met with President Eisenhower at the president's weekend residence, Camp David. They discussed obstacles to peace and agreed to hold a summit meeting in Paris the following May to discuss with leaders of France and Britain how to reduce the danger of war. Eisenhower accepted an invitation to visit the Soviet Union following that summit meeting.

Just before the meeting in Paris, a U.S. reconnaissance plane called the U-2 was spotted over Soviet territory and shot down. At the meeting, Khrushchev asked Eisenhower for an apology for sending the spy plane. Eisenhower refused to apologize; Khrushchev withdrew his invitation for the president to visit the Soviet Union and left the meeting. In October of that same year, 1960, Khrushchev again traveled to the United States to address the meeting of the United Nations General Assembly in New York. There he again protested the U-2 spy plane and, in a gesture reported around the world, took off his shoe and pounded on the table with it to show his anger.

The spy plane was only a minor threat compared to new technologies both nations were testing. Rockets could carry nuclear explosives to targets thousands of miles away. On October 4, 1957, a Soviet rocket had put a small radio transmitter into orbit around the earth. Named *Sputnik*, Russian for "traveling companion," this tiny, unmanned spaceship was Earth's first artificial satellite. In 1961 a larger rocket put a capsule into orbit carrying Soviet cosmonaut Yury Gagarin, the first man in space. These two feats created a demand for matching achievements by the United States, and President John F. Kennedy announced a goal of putting an American astronaut on the moon by 1970. A race to the moon had begun. Space flights can be used for scientific research, for spying, or for attacks. Both superpowers pledged to make peaceful uses of space, but no one was sure those pledges would be kept.

Even though Khrushchev's policies brought some improvements in the life of the ordinary citizen, the standard of living in the Soviet Union was still much lower than that in Western Europe. Political freedom was almost unknown, since one party controlled the government and won every election. As a result, many people wanted to emigrate from the Soviet Union to find a new life in another country. Such ambitions were considered disloyal by earnest Communists, and emigration was strictly forbidden. Every Soviet citizen was expected to work on the traditional Marxist goal of building socialism. But some brave men and women took the risk of leaving the Soviet Union anyway. Some who were lucky enough to be allowed to travel outside the country on business or in cultural exchanges simply went to American embassies and asked for protection. Two who received very warm welcomes in the West were the ballet stars Rudolf Nureyev in 1961 and Mikhail Baryshnikov in 1974.

Others who wanted to leave went to Communist East Germany, where they tried to make their way across the guarded border with West Germany without being seen. Citizens in the satellite countries also sought to emigrate to the West. A popular place for such attempts was Berlin, a bustling city located well behind the iron curtain but still occupied in its western sections by American, British, and French troops. So many East Germans were crossing into the western side and not coming back that Khrushchev decided to put a stop to it. Always one for direct action, in August 1961 he had a wall built to separate East Berlin from West Berlin—a wall with barbed wire on top and guard towers. The similarity to a prison wall did not go unnoticed. The western nations protested the wall and pointed out it was an indication of the failure of communism to provide for people's needs. But the wall stayed in place until 1989.

SOVIET LEADERS STILL BELIEVED COMMUNISM WAS SUPERIOR TO capitalism, and continued to try to persuade other nations of that. In 1959, on the island of Cuba, ninety miles off the coast of Florida, revolutionary leader Fidel Castro had set up a new government. The Soviet Union gave Castro economic help, which he badly needed. Castro chose to follow the Communist model for his country and in 1960 seized a number of industrial plants on the island to be run by the government. Many of these were owned by companies in the United States. Castro rejected diplomatic protests. Many Cubans fled to Florida.

Ballet star Rudolf Nureyev, one of many Soviet artists to seek a new home in the United States, walks on Fifth Avenue in New York with Jacqueline Kennedy.
National Archives

In Washington, the Central Intelligence Agency (CIA) conceived a plan to overthrow Castro with the help of some of the Cubans who had fled the country. The United States would provide boats for them to invade Cuba. The CIA believed that thousands of other Cubans would join them as soon as they landed. When John F. Kennedy was inaugurated president in January 1961 the CIA presented the plan to him and he approved it. The place chosen for the invasion was called the Bay of Pigs. But when the invaders landed in April they got no support from people on the island and were quickly captured by Castro's forces.

Castro asked the Soviet Union for military aid to resist another U.S. invasion. In October 1962 aerial reconnaissance photos showed that the Soviets had set up missile bases in Cuba, with missiles capable of destroying a number of American cities. President Kennedy sent the U.S. Navy to blockade all shipping to Cuba and demanded that the missiles be removed. At first Khrushchev bluntly refused. The situation was so tense that many historians consider these days the closest approach ever to World War III. But neither side wanted war, and after a few days Khrushchev removed the missiles.

The Cuban missile crisis left both the superpowers badly shaken. They realized that both had enough atomic weapons to destroy not only each other but also the whole planet many times over. Though leaders of both countries had pledged never to use atomic weapons, both countries were still testing new ones—to be used "only for defense in case of attack," they said. But this arms race to manufacture and store doomsday weapons created a terrible risk of some sort of accident. Technicians installed a special telephone hot line to allow instant communication between the Kremlin and the White House. In July 1963 the United States and the Soviet Union signed treaties banning the testing of nuclear weapons on land, underwater, or in space. But the treaty did not cover tests underground, and as the memory of the Cuban crisis dimmed, the arms race began again.

In the decade of the 1960s the influence of both superpowers shrank as other nations gained strength. In 1960 the People's Republic of China broke off diplomatic relations with the Soviet Union because it seemed Khrushchev was becoming too friendly with the United States. The nations of Western Europe grew less inclined to take suggestions from Washington. The same was true of Japan, on its way to building the second largest economy in the world. These changed conditions brought a new reasonableness to American-Soviet relations. For example, in 1963 the Soviets had a shortage of wheat and American farmers had a surplus. The Soviets offered to buy their wheat, and the Americans agreed.

By 1963, after ten years in power, Khrushchev had accomplished quite a lot by reducing international dangers. But his policies at home

In 1967, during a thaw in the cold war, Soviet leader Aleksey Kosygin met with U.S. president Lyndon Johnson in Glassboro, New Jersey.
National Archives

had been less successful. Factories were producing more goods for everyday use, but they were of poor quality. The American wheat purchase was seen as a confession of the failure of his agricultural policies. So in 1964 other leaders of the Communist party forced him to resign as First Secretary.

The man chosen to be the new First Secretary was Leonid Brezhnev. The new chairman of the Council of Ministers was Aleksey Kosygin. These two sought to reorganize and improve industrial production. But today the Brezhnev era is regarded in the Soviet Union as the Era of Stagnation. The two new leaders did achieve, however, additional improvements in international relations. They negotiated treaties with the United States for more cultural exchanges of musicians, dancers, and other artists, and a treaty on the peaceful uses of space. In June 1967 Kosygin met with U.S. president Lyndon Johnson at Glassboro State Teachers College in New Jersey and restated a goal of "peaceful coexistence." In 1969 the superpowers began a series of Strategic Arms Limitation Talks (SALT), held in Helsinki, Finland.

Both nations kept the promise not to use nuclear weapons, even during the most serious conflict of the 1960s, the war for control of the former French colony of Vietnam. The Soviet Union backed the Communist armies of General Ho Chi Minh, and the United States backed the armies resisting the Communists.

By 1968 half a million American soldiers were fighting in Vietnam. But the elected officials that the Americans supported failed to win the allegiance of a majority of the Vietnamese citizens. The country had been torn by war ever since 1941. Finally, in 1969, President Richard Nixon recognized that the situation was hopeless and began to bring American ground troops home. With the collapse of South Vietnam in 1975, the Communists established a government for all of Vietnam.

As THE WITHDRAWAL FROM VIETNAM INDICATES, PRESIDENT Nixon brought a new realism to U.S. foreign policy, long based on lofty statements of unattainable goals and vehement denunciations of opposing political theories. Nixon and his secretary of state, Henry Kissinger, visited both Communist giants, the Soviet Union and the People's Republic of China. The Strategic Arms Limitation Talks, begun in 1969, produced a first agreement (SALT I), which Brezhnev and Nixon signed in 1971. Other talks on the subject of cooperation between nations and protection of basic human rights led to agreements signed in 1975 by thirty-five nations. The agreements are known as the Helsinki Accords from the location of the talks.

Protection of basic human rights was discussed more and more in the Soviet Union. Two of the most effective voices were those of nuclear physicist Andrey Sakharov and his wife, Yelena Bonner. Dr. Sakharov had played a principal role in the development of the Soviet hydrogen bomb but then had tried to persuade his government to stop nuclear testing. His interest broadened from the right to free speech on the subject of disarmament to the right to criticize all government policies, and from there to a concern for all human rights. In 1970 he was a leader in the formation in the Soviet Union of the Committee on Human Rights, which called attention to violations of those rights by the government. His work was recognized by the award of the Nobel Peace Prize in 1975, but he was refused a visa to go to Oslo to accept it. Yelena Bonner went in his place and read the call for freedom he had written in his acceptance speech. His international reputation as a physicist protected him until 1980. In that year his vigorous protests of government actions caused him to be sent from Moscow to the city of Gorky, into modern exile, cut off from communication with the world. Even there he served as a rallying point, a clear example of the gap between government words at Helsinki and deeds at home. A group calling itself Helsinki Watch began pointing out other examples.

The year 1979, ending a decade that began with several movements in the direction of world peace, saw new wars on the southern borders of the Soviet Union. The population of the region around the Caspian Sea and the Persian Gulf is largely Muslim, but sharply divided into various sects. In the Soviet Union itself, Muslims numbered fifty-five million, more than one-sixth of the total population, most of them living in the southern Soviet republics that border on Muslim nations. This same region produces a large part of the world's oil supply, at prices no other source can match. Religion and oil are both powerful incentives to war.

Most of the region's oil production was developed in the years 1908–1938. In the Soviet Union state enterprises pumped and shipped the oil. Production in the other nations of the region was developed by oil companies based in Europe and the United States. These other oil-producing nations were centuries-old monarchies, ruled according to Muslim religious beliefs, the law of Islam. As the wealth generated by oil allowed economic development and modernization, the monarchs sent students abroad to study, to learn how to manage the changes. It was inevitable that economic change would also lead to suggestions for political change: constitutions, elected representatives, more freedom for women—changes made in Europe at least a century earlier. In most of the Muslim nations such suggestions made small progress against the strong force of traditional religion. But by the decade of the 1970s enough changes had occurred in some of the nations for Muslim religious leaders to be alarmed and call for an Islamic resurgence, a return to the days when Islam alone determined the law of the land. The call was heard by Muslims everywhere, including those in the Soviet Union, who had suffered along with Christians and Jews from Communist opposition to all religion.

The Muslim nation that had strayed the farthest from the path of Islam was Iran, where in 1925 an army officer with modern ideas made himself shah. By 1978 his son, Mohammad Reza Pahlavi, was opposed both by Muslim leaders, who felt his program to modernize the nation was a threat to religious values, and by intellectuals, who resented his curbs on free discussion of political ideas. In January 1979 his combined opponents drove the shah from his throne, to be replaced as ruler by a fundamentalist Muslim leader, the ayatollah Ruholla Khomeini. The ayatollah soon made it clear that he was eager to encourage Islamic resurgence among the Muslim populations of all countries.

Brezhnev had barely digested that unwelcome news from the south when he received more. In September 1980 Iran's neighbor Iraq, believing the new government weak, invaded Iran, beginning a long war. The Soviet Union joined many other nations in denouncing this threat to stability in the Persian Gulf area.

Meanwhile, in the mountainous nation of Afghanistan, situated between the Soviet Union, Iran, and Pakistan, another government was overthrown. In April 1978 a group of Marxist military men set up the People's Democratic Republic of Afghanistan and signed a treaty of friendship with the Soviet Union. But no government has ever really controlled the Afghan mountain tribesmen. These independent men resented Marxist efforts to purge their Muslim religious leaders and began to wage guerrilla war on the new regime. The guerrillas called themselves *mujaheddin,* meaning "holy warriors." The Marxists, weakened by conflicts among themselves, repeatedly asked the Soviet Union for military help to stay in power. In December 1979 Brezhnev sent Soviet forces into Afghanistan. He pointed out he was doing so at the request of the Afghan government, which was literally true, but the rest of the world viewed the action as an invasion intended to expand Soviet power. This view was confirmed when the Afghan president was assassinated the day after the troops arrived and replaced by a man Brezhnev chose. In January the United Nations General Assembly censured Brezhnev's sending troops by a vote of 104–18. Muslim soldiers, who make up much of the Soviet army, were naturally reluctant to fight against fellow

Muslims in Afghanistan. In the Soviet republics with large Muslim populations, discontent with rule from Moscow grew.

U.S. president Jimmy Carter called Russian control of Afghanistan a possible "stepping-stone" toward Soviet control of Persian Gulf oil supplies. He halted shipments of wheat and high-tech equipment from the United States to the Soviet Union. He also struck a blow at Soviet pride. Moscow had been chosen as host of the 1980 Olympic Games, the powerful symbol of peaceful competition among nations. Work was going forward on facilities to accommodate the thousands of athletes and spectators who would visit the Soviet Union, most of them for the first time. President Carter announced that U.S. athletes would not participate in the Games in Moscow and urged other nations to boycott the Games also. Physicist Andrey Sakharov issued a similar plea, denouncing the invasion. That was the action that caused him to be exiled to Gorky.

The Afghan tribesmen fought against the Soviet troops just as tenaciously as against all previous foes. The principal military effect of Soviet aid was to cause half the army of the Afghan government to defect to the guerrillas. But the effect on the civilian population was devastating, as Soviet guns and planes destroyed towns and villages. About 800,000 Afghans, out of a population estimated at 22,450,000, fled across the mountains into Pakistan. As the war continued, the United States began sending weapons to the *mujaheddin* guerrillas. In time Soviet intervention in Afghanistan would be compared to U.S. intervention in Vietnam: a war unpopular with citizens back home, but difficult to end once begun.

By 1980 COMMUNIST GOVERNMENTS HAD RULED THE NATIONS of Eastern Europe for thirty-five years. They had succeeded in building a military force equal to that of the North Atlantic Treaty Organization. In some areas, most notably exploration of outer space, Soviet accomplishments surpassed those of all other nations. But for ordinary people, Communist promises of a workers' paradise had hardly been met at all. Food was scarce or expensive or both; clothing and housing were of poor quality. Worse, for many, was control of national life by only one political party, and that one directed from Moscow. Discussion of alternatives to communism was suppressed. And practice of religion, though allowed, was discouraged and strictly controlled.

While the government could regulate religious activities—church services, schools, printing of Bibles—it could not regulate religious belief. Parents passed their faith on to their children. As in other times of persecution, many believers found their faith strengthened by the hardships and dangers they faced.

In Poland the vast majority of the population has been devoutly Roman Catholic for centuries. Polish bishops and archbishops steadfastly preserved the influence of the church. Particularly effective was the archbishop of Krakow, Karol Cardinal Wojtyla. In October 1978, when Pope John Paul I died, the College of Cardinals in Rome elected Cardinal Wojtyla the new pope. He took the name John Paul II.

It was the first time that the cardinals had elected a pope who was Polish. The effect on all Poles was enormous. The following year, in June 1979, Pope John Paul returned to his native land for a nine-day visit. He was welcomed by huge crowds. He urged Polish bishops to continue their defense of the rights of the church against government control.

In 1980 Polish pride in the new pope joined with discontent with the standard of living under communism. The Polish bishops declared that the people should be free to form organizations not controlled by the state: religious organizations and other organizations as well. Workers in a number of cities demanded permission to form independent labor unions to replace the unions controlled by the Communist party. Surprisingly, the government listened.

The most effective leader of the Polish workers was an electrician, Lech Walesa, employed at the shipyard in the port city of Gdansk (formerly called Danzig). Walesa organized Solidarity, a nationwide federation of independent labor unions that included about half of all workers in the country. A strike called by Solidarity could affect all of Poland.

Similar acts of independence had brought Soviet troops to Hungary and to Czechoslovakia. Many expected tanks to roll into Poland. Brezhnev knew how world opinion would react to that. So he sent troops toward the Polish border but not across it. That had the desired effect, at least for a time. The Polish government declared martial law, squelched many of the new independent organizations, and put Lech Walesa and many other leaders of Solidarity in jail.

Brezhnev praised these measures, without which, he said, "the stability of Europe and even of the world at large would have been at risk." He was right about the threat to stability, as imposed from Moscow. But he was wrong to think martial law in Poland had ended that threat. Brezhnev's policies that had produced the Era of Stagnation were now being challenged in all the satellite countries, and also in the Soviet Union itself. Brezhnev himself was ill. In 1982, at age seventy-six, he died.

There followed three years in which the political expression *the old guard* had its literal meaning. The man chosen to succeed Brezhnev as general secretary of the Central Committee of the Communist party was Yuri Andropov, age sixty-eight. Andropov died two years later, to be succeeded by Konstantin Chernenko, age seventy-two. Chernenko lived to complete only one year in office.

Finally, in 1985, when Chernenko died, the Central Committee recognized the time had come to turn the leadership of the nation over to the next generation. They elected as general secretary an energetic agricultural expert from the southern region between the Caspian and Black seas, comparatively young at fifty-four. His many friends and his wife, a lecturer at Moscow State University, called him Mischa. His formal name is Mikhail Gorbachev. A few observers noted that he was the first head of state in Moscow named Mikhail, Russian for Michael, since the first Romanov czar, the grandfather of Peter the Great. They asked if General Secretary Mikhail Gorbachev and his generation would bring as many changes as the Romanovs had.

CHAPTER TEN

GORBACHEV, NEW THINKING, AND A NEW GOVERNMENT

$\mathfrak{M}$IKHAIL SERGEYEVICH GORBACHEV WAS BORN ON MARCH 2, 1931, in the village of Privolnoe, between the Black and Caspian seas, just north of the Caucasus Mountains. The area is famous for its scenery, with flat grassland—the Russian steppes—extending toward snow-capped peaks. Until the eighteenth century cossack horsemen rode these steppes free of control from the czar on anyone. After Czar Alexander II built a fortress in 1777 Russians settled around it. Writers including Pushkin and Tolstoy wrote about the beauty of the land and the free way of life still enjoyed by its people. In time the region became popular for vacations for the czarist nobility and after them the Communist commissars. When the Soviet Union was formed the area was named the Stavropol Territory, for its principal city.

The Gorbachev family were farmers. Men, women, and children all worked the land and grew enough for their needs. But soon after Mikhail was born the great change to government-run collective farms reached as far as Privolnoe. Farmers who resisted this change were arrested and sent off to work in labor camps, usually in Siberia.

Someone in Privolnoe accused Andrey Gorbachev, Mikhail's grandfather, of holding back some wheat from the government's agents. Perhaps he wanted to be sure his family would be fed, or perhaps he wanted to be sure to have seed wheat to plant in the fall, or perhaps the accusation was completely false. In any event, Andrey Gorbachev was sent off to Siberia for nine years. Of course Mikhail never forgot that or the terrible famine Stalin's agricultural policy caused.

Another action by the Gorbachev family would also have displeased the government, but it was kept a secret. They had Mikhail baptized in the Russian Orthodox faith. Practice of religion was not prohibited by the Communists, but it was definitely discouraged, and no church schools were allowed. But religion was an integral part of the culture Mikhail absorbed as a boy. In the public school he was a good student, interested in many things. Along with reading and writing and the rest, he took the required courses in Communist doctrine. When he was old enough he joined the Communist youth organization Komsomol.

In 1941, when Mikhail was ten, Hitler invaded the Soviet Union. Mikhail's father and older brother both served in the army. His brother died in battle in 1943. His father took part in driving the Germans out and back into Poland.

As the war ended in 1945, Mikhail, age fourteen, joined his mother and the other women and boys of Privolnoe working on the collective farm. He helped the man who operated the tractor combine that harvested the wheat. But he continued to go to school and continued to do well there.

A university education was available free to the best students in the Soviet Union, and for the best of the best, an education at Moscow State University. Mikhail was awarded that top honor. He arrived in Moscow, along with hundreds of other bright young men and women from across the nation, in the fall of 1950. As soon as he opened his mouth he was recognized as a southerner. As soon as he had said a few sentences, he was recognized as a charming person. He possessed a great sense of humor and an eager curiosity about new ideas.

Immediately he had to choose which school of the university he would enroll in. He chose the School of Law, a five-year course at Moscow State. And the School of Law chose him as the *komsorg*—Komsomol organizer—for the freshman class. His career in Communist party politics had begun on the bottom rung of a very long ladder. Later he was named *komsorg* of the whole School of Law. His responsibilities were not heavy, leaving plenty of time for studies, dormitory bull sessions, and social life. All those activities had a great effect on his future.

One of the students who had the most interesting things to say, in bull sessions and in private conversation, was Zdenek Mlynar, a young man from Czechoslovakia. The Soviet Union encouraged large numbers of students from other countries to pursue their education in the capital of communism. But in 1950 Communists had controlled Czechoslovakia for only five years, and there were still many people there who were talking about the country's former democracy and freedom. So the young Czech brought a lot of information about alternate ways of governing, for anyone who was interested. Mikhail was interested, and the two became good friends.

Another student who had an even greater influence on Mikhail's future was a beautiful young woman named Raisa Titorenko. She was not only beautiful, she had been the top student in her high school in Sterlitamak, just west of the Ural Mountains. She had come to study philosophy at Moscow State. She and Mikhail met, and soon the two students from small country towns were exploring the big city together, attending the theater, searching through the bookstores and libraries. In their senior year they were married, and after graduation Mikhail took Raisa to live in Stavropol.

The young law graduate did not practice law but took a job with the Komsomol youth group in Stavropol. Gradually he climbed up the political ladder. Work with the youth organization could not go on forever, so he decided to get another degree, in agriculture this time, at night school at the Stavropol Agricultural Institute. Raisa also decided to work for another degree. Still keeping pace with each other, in 1967 Mikhail got his degree and Raisa submitted her doctoral dissertation to the Lenin Pedagogical Institute in Moscow. Its title was "The Emergence of New Characteristics in the Daily Life of Collective Farm Peasantry (Based on Sociological Investigation in the Stavropol Territory)."

The attractive, energetic couple won the respect of Fyodor Kulakov, First Secretary of the Communist party in Stavropol, who moved Mikhail from youth work to local party headquarters. By 1970 Kulakov had been promoted to the national government in Moscow as secretary for agriculture, and Mikhail succeeded him as party First Secretary in Stavropol.

The beautiful area north of the Caucasus Mountains was still popular for vacations of high-ranking members of the government. Mikhail Gorbachev's new office made him their official host, a role he enjoyed and one that also gave him some powerful acquaintances. Most powerful was Yuri Andropov, for many years head of the KGB, the Committee for National Security. Those initials mean to most Americans a Soviet equivalent of the CIA, with a secret police branch added. Actually the KGB had much broader responsibilities, and Andropov was not a villain out of a James Bond movie but an able and forward-looking government administrator. By the time he met Gorbachev he was frustrated by the policies adopted by the Kremlin under Communist party chief Brezhnev and was looking for bright younger men to help him bring an end to the Era of Stagnation. Kulakov called Gorbachev to his attention, and over the course of several vacations Andropov decided he was the sort of man he needed.

When Kulakov died, Andropov suggested to Brezhnev that Gorbachev be the new secretary for agriculture. Brezhnev took his vacations even farther south than Stavropol, but Andropov arranged for his train to stop en route long enough for him to meet Gorbachev. The interview stretched out to two hours, and Gorbachev got the job.

Brezhnev died in 1982 and Andropov got the top Kremlin office. But he was already seriously ill when he was inaugurated, and he died in 1984, before he could insure that Gorbachev would succeed him. His actual successor, Konstantin Chernenko, died in 1985. Three deaths of the head of state in four years had made it clear it was time to pass the leadership on to a younger generation.

MIKHAIL GORBACHEV WAS ELECTED GENERAL SECRETARY OF THE Central Committee of the Communist party of the Soviet Union on March 11, 1985. He took command of a nation with many recent accomplishments and many long-standing problems. The Soviet space station *Salyut 7*—the Russian word meaning "salute"—had been orbiting the earth for almost three years. On it, cosmonauts broke record after record for living in space, with one pair staying on board for 237 days. A new pipeline was bringing natural gas from Siberia to supply not only Soviet needs but also those of Western Europe, earning $8 billion a year and at the same time building commercial relations. And construction of the new railroad across Siberia, the Baikal-Amur Mainline, or BAM, was providing a great boost to the economic development of that vast and mineral-rich province, with the promise of benefits for the whole nation. There was reason for optimism. Gorbachev, at fifty-four the youngest

Soviet head of state since Joseph Stalin won control after the death of Lenin in 1924, was a man who looked to the future.

The present was a much less happy picture. Hanging over all was the worry that the stockpiles of nuclear weapons built up by both the Soviet Union and the United States might bring life on earth to an end, wiping out the future altogether. If that catastrophe could be avoided there was still the huge cost of engaging in an arms race with the other superpower. Closer to home, there was the human cost of fighting a war in Afghanistan, where thousands of young men were being killed or crippled every month.

Then there were less dramatic but no less difficult problems in everyday life. Collective farms were not producing enough food to feed 281 million citizens, and food had to be imported, even though the Soviet Union has vast expanses of some of the world's most fertile farmland. Factories were turning out goods of poor quality. Underlying these production problems were a high rate of alcoholism among Soviet males and serious defects in the educational system.

To deal with all these problems at home and abroad General Secretary Gorbachev proposed three new government policies: *glasnost,* meaning "openness," *perestroika,* meaning "restructuring," and *demokratizatsiya,* meaning "democratization." *Glasnost* came first. Soviet citizens were encouraged to speak their opinions openly, including opinions critical of the government and of the Communist party that ran it. Journalists were allowed more freedom to pursue stories. More Soviet cities were opened to visitors from other countries. More motion pictures from abroad were allowed to be shown. Rock music, long declared a sample of "Western decadence," was allowed, and Billy Joel and other rock musicians conducted successful concert tours in the Soviet Union.

A nineteen-year-old amateur pilot from West Germany, Mathias Rust, flew his small plane from Finland all the way to Moscow without being stopped by the Soviet air force, and landed in Red Square outside the Kremlin wall. He was arrested, tried, and sentenced to four years in a labor camp, a sentence later reduced. But world opinion was astonished that he was not shot out of the air. The Soviet defense minister was immediately replaced.

There had always been some brave men and women like Andrey Sakharov and Yelena Bonner criticizing government policy even though it meant exile or worse. To spread their ideas they had depended on *samizdat* (meaning "self-publishing"), using creaky duplicating machines hidden in basements and attics, and on an underground distribution network. Now their words were printed openly. Gorbachev telephoned Sakharov in Gorky and told him he was free to return to Moscow. The new general secretary sincerely wanted openness, and soon lively debates were going on all over the nation.

Perestroika, or restructuring of the economy, was a more difficult goal. Gorbachev spelled out his ideas in a book published in a number of countries including the United States, entitled *Perestroika: New Thinking for Our Country and the World.* The book attracted wide attention because of the author's expressed willingness to break with the past and because of his common sense compared to the pompous theories of many politicians.

Yet, as one Soviet observer said, "It is easier to print a book than to make salami." Some westerners said what the Soviet Union needed was to throw out the whole Communist structure of state ownership and build a free-enterprise economy. But Gorbachev had come to power as general secretary of the Central Committee of the Communist party. He said the problem was not communism, but the distortions of communism that had occurred in the nearly seventy years since the revolution. The solution, he said, was to return to the basic teachings of the father of his country, V. I. Lenin.

Gorbachev was a master of public relations. Instead of posting his own picture all over the nation, as former leaders had done, he posted pictures of Lenin. And under them were not Gorbachev's words, but Lenin's—carefully chosen, of course, to make the points Gorbachev wanted made.

The words of Lenin that interested Gorbachev most concerned the New Economic Policy of 1921, a backing away from pure communism to introduce a bit of capitalist incentive to produce more. As Gorbachev explained, Karl Marx had a goal for the relation of the worker to the state: "From each according to his ability, to each according to his need." Lenin had adjusted this to read: "From each according to his ability, to each according to his work." Gorbachev gave managers of factories and collective farms more freedom to decide how they would arrange their affairs, with less direction from Moscow, but with the accompanying requirement that they be held accountable for the results. He allowed a quarter of the land in collective farms to be assigned to families, who could use it any way they chose. He also allowed citizens to form cooperatives—small, independent businesses such as restaurants and vegetable markets.

Perestroika required major changes in the way people worked— changes difficult for most workers to accept. To assist him in pressing for reform Gorbachev brought to Moscow a towering six-foot Siberian, Boris Yeltsin. The two men were born in the same year and met when both were district party chiefs, Gorbachev in Stavropol and Yeltsin in the Sverdlovsk District in the Ural Mountains. Gorbachev knew that Yeltsin had worked effectively to end corruption and introduce reforms in Sverdlovsk. He named him Communist party First Secretary for the city of Moscow, and a candidate member of the Politburo.

Boris Yeltsin accepted his double assignment with enthusiasm. In Moscow he startled the party rank and file by turning up in stores and plants and party offices, demanding facts, firing the incompetent, arresting the corrupt. But he also startled the Politburo by speaking out in meetings to demand a faster pace of reform in the national government. By 1987 Yeltsin's sharp criticisms caused Gorbachev to dismiss him from both his posts.

Gorbachev's own technique was quite different from Yeltsin's bullying. Gorbachev lectured and cajoled. He took his program directly to the people, traveling through the nation, speaking to the man in the street, shaking hands, seeking popular support for his policies. Two of his often repeated themes were "Work harder" and "Drink less."

To discourage excessive drinking Gorbachev reduced the hours liquor stores were open and raised the price of vodka, the national drink, by 33 percent. That approach did not succeed. A shortage of sugar suddenly developed, as thirsty Soviets began to distill their own bootleg vodka. Admitting his failure, Gorbachev reversed his decrees and continued campaigning for less drinking.

The rest of the world watched the new Soviet leader with fascination. That was made easy by *glasnost*. And only months after he took office Gorbachev began visiting the capitals of the world: London, Paris, Washington, Beijing, Berlin, Warsaw. Like all his predecessors, he spoke of the desire of his government for peace.

Soon President Ronald Reagan announced that the United States would abide by the terms of the 1979 Strategic Arms Limitation Treaty (SALT II), even though it had not yet been ratified by the Senate. The two leaders agreed that they would go to Geneva for a summit meeting in November 1985. Then in September Gorbachev made major new proposals for reducing the danger of war.

Gorbachev announced that the Soviet Union would reduce the number of its nuclear weapons by 50 percent if President Reagan would slow development of one of his favorite projects, the Strategic Defense Initiative (SDI). This project proposed a shield in orbit over the earth that would detect and destroy missiles launched on rockets from any nation. Because of the extremely sophisticated technology required to be developed to create the shield, the SDI project was nicknamed Star Wars, after the popular George Lucas film about combat in space. President Reagan believed SDI would make all missiles useless and thus be worth the enormous cost of developing it. Other leaders, including Gorbachev, feared that the shield, even though it was built for defense, could serve as a base in space for an attack. As such, it was viewed as a major increase in the U.S. weapons stockpile.

Despite the disagreement over Star Wars, Reagan and Gorbachev went ahead with the summit meeting in Geneva. The major result was that they became acquainted person to person.

On April 26, 1986, the world got a terrible sample of the horror of a nuclear explosion. At Chernobyl in Ukraine, seventy miles north of Kiev, a plant generating electricity from nuclear power exploded, fatally injuring thirty-one people and sending a cloud of radioactive material into the atmosphere. Winds spread this material across Europe all the way to the Atlantic, making crops unsafe to eat for man or animal. Cows grazing on grass affected by the fallout gave radioactive milk. In the following months and years many more people in Ukraine died as a result of exposure to the radioactivity.

The disaster was a severe test of Gorbachev's new openness. The Soviet government waited two days before announcing the explosion. In past disasters the government had refused aid offered by other countries. But coping with a nuclear disaster required the expertise of all the world. The Soviet government allowed international teams of experts to fly to Chernobyl—engineers to develop ways to contain the runaway reactor and physicians to treat the patients dying of radiation sickness. These men of science reported what they saw and called on the people of the world to rise above national politics and act to remove the nuclear threat to Earth.

General Secretary Gorbachev and President Reagan met again, in October 1986, in Reykjavík, Iceland. Proposals for arms reductions were made more specific. The talks did not resolve the strong difference of opinion of the two men concerning the Star Wars missile shield, but the negotiations on disarmament continued. Finally in 1987 the two sides agreed that both would reduce the number of their nuclear weapons of the size called "intermediate." Both nations retained enough other weapons to destroy each other and the planet many times over, but this agreement was the first that promised reduction rather than just limitation. In December 1987 Gorbachev traveled to Washington to sign the agreement.

It was the first visit to the United States by a Soviet head of state since General Secretary Brezhnev visited President Nixon in 1973. The American people were eager to see for themselves this man who had been charming audiences in so many nations. Gorbachev invited what he called "a cross section of American opinion leaders" to meet with him for an hour, and few refused the invitation. To the dismay of the Secret Service detail responsible for his safety, he halted his automobile on a Washington street crowded with pedestrians at the lunch hour and shook hands with a number of them. The general reaction on that street was pleased surprise.

In April 1988 representatives of Afghanistan, the Soviet Union, the United States, and Pakistan announced agreement on the withdrawal of Soviet troops from Afghanistan. This withdrawal was completed the following February.

In 1988 President Reagan visited the Soviet Union and walked arm in arm with Gorbachev across the square in the Kremlin. Television coverage before and during the visit gave the American people their most complete look up to that time at the nation they had so long been told was their chief enemy.

Many other Americans visited the Soviet Union that year to participate in the celebration of the thousand-year anniversary of the adoption of Christianity by Prince Vladimir of Kiev in 988, the date considered the beginning of the national church. Many church properties that had been seized by the state after the revolution were returned, including one in Kiev that had been converted into the Museum of Atheism.

Shortly after the Reagan visit, five thousand delegates met in Moscow in June 1988 for the Nineteenth All-Union Conference of the Communist

President Ronald Reagan speaks to an audience of university students in Moscow in May 1988, at the time of his fourth summit meeting.
Bill Fitz-Patrick, the White House

party. The party conference, the first since 1941, was quite different from a party congress, which had been little more than a rubber stamp to approve the actions and policies of the Politburo. Gorbachev convened the conference, he said, to consider a "complete overhaul" of the nation's political structure in order to make it work better. In an atmosphere of surprising frankness delegates from all over the Soviet Union questioned and criticized government actions. Most notable was the delegate from Moscow, Boris Yeltsin. Though his criticisms of the slow pace of reform had cost him his position as chief of the Communist party in Moscow, he was enormously popular with ordinary citizens, and at the conference he continued to speak out. The party-controlled newspaper *Pravda* published a long interview with him while the conference was still meeting—a major departure from past reporting of party business, which told only of unanimous votes of approval.

Even a "complete overhaul" of government would make little difference as long as the Communist party had all the power to make decisions. Gorbachev was too clever a politician to suggest in 1988 that the party as well as the government might have its faults. But developments in later years showed he was quite aware of that. At the conference he proposed to reduce the bureaucracy that was responsible for the stagnation that had prevailed since the days of Brezhnev. To accomplish this he proposed a new constitution that would give more power to the elected representatives of the people. That was the same promise made by Czar Alexander II just before he was assassinated in 1881, and by Lenin in 1917 for some future year when the revolution was firmly established.

Specifically, the proposed constitution would establish a new parliament, called the Congress of People's Deputies. Of its 2,250 members, 1,500 would be chosen by a nationwide election and 750 by the Communist party and other organizations. This parliament would meet once a year and elect the 450 members of the Supreme Soviet. The Supreme Soviet would be responsible for making laws. The constitution also created a new office, president of the Union of Soviet Socialist Republics. This president was to be elected not by nationwide balloting but by the parliament.

Elections for the new parliament were held in March 1989. It was permitted for the ballots to list more than one candidate for each seat. When the votes were counted many non-Communists won, and twenty prominent party members had the novel experience of losing an election. One of the new deputies elected was Andrey Sakharov. Another was Boris Yeltsin.

In December 1988 Gorbachev made his second visit to the United States. In a speech to the General Assembly of the United Nations on December 7 he announced further arms reductions. That same day a major earthquake hit the Soviet Republic of Armenia. Gorbachev immediately returned home to visit Armenia and plan help. The quake had killed about twenty-five thousand people, had left half a million people homeless, and had caused at least $8 billion in property damage. As after the Chernobyl nuclear power plant disaster, the government allowed aid teams from other nations to help. Some of the most severely injured victims were airlifted to the United States for special medical attention.

Relations with the West were improving. Gorbachev wanted to improve relations also with his neighbor on the east, the other major Communist power, the People's Republic of China. In May 1989 he visited Beijing to shake hands with the Chinese leadership.

Chinese university students welcomed him with banners calling for democracy in China similar to what Gorbachev was introducing at home. The welcome soon grew into a demonstration as thousands of students filled Tienanmen Square—"Square of the Gate of Heavenly Peace." International television crews, already in Beijing to cover the Gorbachev visit, sent pictures of the demonstration to viewers all over the world.

After Gorbachev left China, many of the demonstrators returned to their classes. But enough remained in Tienanmen Square to cause the government to send troops to clear the area by force. On the night of Saturday, June 3, 1989, military units opened fire on the students, and hundreds of students and soldiers died in confused fighting. The Tienanmen massacre damaged China's relations with all the rest of the world and began a new period of repression by its Communist government. Gorbachev made no direct comment on the massacre but later in the year sent only a minimal delegation to the celebration of the fortieth anniversary of the founding of the People's Republic of China.

The new parliament met in Moscow in May 1989 and to no one's surprise chose General Secretary Gorbachev the first president of the Union of Soviet Socialist Republics. The head of the Communist party was still the head of state, no matter what actual titles he had. But like the Nineteenth All-Union Conference a year earlier, the first meeting of the new parliament was marked by frankness of debate and admission of serious problems in the nation.

Frankness went even further. Gorbachev admitted that the other Communist governments in Eastern Europe also had problems, including burdensome layers of bureaucrats. He made it clear that he would not support such governments with Soviet troops and tanks, as his predecessors had done in Hungary and Czechoslovakia when their citizens rose against them. The reforms already achieved in Poland by the joint efforts of the church and the labor union Solidarity were a sample of what could be done.

The second half of 1989 brought a series of changes in Eastern Europe at a pace that surprised everyone. All six of the Communist governments there were driven out of office by reform-minded citizens: in Poland, Hungary, East Germany, Bulgaria, Czechoslovakia, and Romania. The other nations of the world watched in astonishment as, in the journalists' phrase, "the Communist monolith crumbled." Soon invitations were going out from Eastern Europe encouraging capitalist investors to come build factories and even set up stock exchanges.

National borders—long fortified with barbed wire to keep Eastern Europeans from defecting to the West—were opened to free travel. Many families headed west at once, while others waited to see how their native lands would fare in a new era. On November 9, 1989, the most famous barrier of all, the Berlin Wall separating the eastern and western sectors of that city, was broken through. International television cameras were on hand as Berliners celebrated far into the night, climbing over the wall, singing on top of it, pulling bits of it apart with hammers and bare hands. Before long some of the more enterprising celebrants realized the pieces would make valuable souvenirs to sell in the shops.

The end of the Berlin Wall was a symbol that the cold war was over. As Gorbachev said, it had been an enormously costly war for both sides: "The cold war has ended, or is ending, not because there are victors and vanquished but because there is neither one nor the other." But now the way was clear to devote the resources of the nations to a period of peace.

In December 1989 Gorbachev met with President George Bush to discuss ongoing efforts to reduce armaments and proposals for increased economic cooperation between the Soviet Union and Western nations. The meetings were held on board ships moored in the harbor of the island of Malta in the Mediterranean. A fierce storm with winds up to sixty miles per hour churned up sixteen-foot seas, causing some rescheduling of the sessions, but the atmosphere below decks was almost joyful, as the leaders exchanged jokes and agreed to meet again the following June.

OPPOSITE:
Berliners celebrate the breakup of the Berlin Wall.
German Information Center

As the 1980s ended, Gorbachev's most serious problems were domestic ones. One such he called "the nationalities problem." The boundaries of the fifteen republics of the Soviet Union corresponded roughly to the homelands of various ethnic groups—the Ukrainians, the Byelorussians, and so on. Armenia, Georgia, Azerbaijan, Estonia, Lithuania, and Latvia had all been independent nations at one time, and their men and women still thought of themselves first as Armenians and Georgians, for example, and only second as Soviet citizens. *Glasnost* gave them the opportunity to call for greater control over their own affairs. To take only two examples, the Armenians demanded that an area in the neighboring Republic of Azerbaijan that is inhabited largely by Armenians be transferred to the Republic of Armenia. The Estonians, Lithuanians, and Latvians had an even larger demand: independence from the Soviet Union.

The three Baltic nations—Estonia, Lithuania, and Latvia—had been added to the Soviet Union in 1940 through agreements between Joseph Stalin and Adolf Hitler. Leaders in these republics pointed out that the agreements had no legality and had never been recognized by other nations.

Gorbachev called on the Baltic leaders to follow constitutional procedure to leave the union. There was a provision for that dating from Lenin's time. They replied that that procedure was too slow.

In Moscow many Communist party officials were alarmed that Gorbachev would even consider allowing republics to leave the union. They called on him to take a hard line, using force if necessary to preserve the nation's strength, and with it their own power and privileges. Six nations in Eastern Europe had seen their Communist governments overthrown as soon as Gorbachev made it clear he would no longer support them with Soviet tanks. The hard-liners did not want to see that happen in the nation that was the standard-bearer of international communism.

Gorbachev was caught between criticisms from two sides. The hard-liners called for strong measures to maintain the power of the central government in Moscow. On the other side, leaders such as Boris Yeltsin said Gorbachev must move more quickly toward needed reforms of that government.

The Communist party had nurtured Gorbachev throughout his career. He still believed it was possible to reform it enough to have it continue as one of several parties in the nation. But the Soviet constitution called the Communist party the "leading and guiding force in Soviet society." Such a one-party monopoly was inconsistent with democracy. Gorbachev persuaded the party's Central Committee that it was necessary to remove that provision from the constitution, and over the vigorous objections of the hard-liners, it was done.

Prodemocracy leaders applauded the word change. Voters in Moscow, Leningrad, and Kiev elected non-Communists to offices in their city governments. In May 1990 Boris Yeltsin ran for president of the largest of the fifteen republics, the Russian republic, and won.

Despite these setbacks for the Communist party, the economic structure of the country was still the structure built by Communist plans. The restructuring, Gorbachev's *perestroika,* was showing few results. Production of food and manufactured goods was not increasing. Government debt was growing.

Gorbachev announced major reductions in the size of the armed forces, with the triple benefit of lessening the dangerous level of world tension, reducing government expenditures, and freeing young men for productive work. He hoped the returning soldiers would join with their families to take advantage of the opportunities he had provided: to take ownership of land from the collective farms and cultivate it, or to start up small cooperatives—businesses independent of the government. But the level of such free-market enterprise stayed surprisingly low.

The crops and the goods that were produced were transported to consumers by a poor transportation system. It has been estimated that as much as a third of the food grown in the Soviet Union spoils on its way to market.

A test of Gorbachev's strength and of his political skill came in July 1990 at the Twenty-eighth Congress of the Communist party. The ten-day congress produced many complaints about problems but few solutions. It was clear at once that the delegates held widely differing views on the pace of change needed. On the very first day a delegate from eastern Siberia called on Gorbachev to resign. Gorbachev suggested that the motion be tabled for later consideration, and it was. He allowed both hard-liners and democrats to be heard. His immediate objective

In May 1990 Soviet president Mikhail Gorbachev made his second visit to Washington to confer with President George Bush.
Joyce C. Naltchayan, the White House

seemed to be to shift the power away from the Communist party to the national government established by the new constitution. Since he was president of that government, his personal power would continue even if the party declined.

On the last day of the congress, Boris Yeltsin asked to speak. In very few words he explained that he intended to devote all his energies to his office as president of the Russian republic. As such, he said, "I cannot fulfill only the instructions of the Communist party. . . . I have to bow to the will of all the people." He resigned from the party and walked out of the session, followed by television cameras. The next day the mayors of Moscow and Leningrad also resigned from the party. Thousands of rank-and-file members turned in their party membership cards.

When the party congress ended in July 1990 Gorbachev still had five years left of his first term as president. It was still true that "it is easier to print a book than to make salami." Gorbachev spent a lot of time in 1990 with his economic advisers, working on a plan to increase production. Their plan provided for much of the property held by the government—housing, factories, farms—to be sold to private citizens or to privately owned companies.

While Gorbachev was wrestling with these domestic problems, an international crisis arose. In August 1990, in the lands just south of the Soviet Union, President Saddam Hussein of Iraq shocked the world by invading his neighboring country, Kuwait. Almost all the nations of the world immediately condemned this act of aggression. The Soviet Union, the United States, and various other nations joined in a United Nations peacekeeping force. For the first time in many years the United Nations Organization was acting effectively—unitedly—to deter aggression. After Hussein ignored repeated appeals, the United Nations force drove the invaders from Kuwait in a month-long air war and one hundred hours of ground combat.

The new spirit of cooperation between the United States and the USSR had a marked effect on the military situation in the whole Middle East. As part of cold war strategy the USSR had been supplying the Arab nations with arms, and the United States had been doing the same for Israel. Now President Gorbachev and President Bush joined in urging all the nations in the Middle East to sit down together at a peace conference sponsored by the superpowers.

In October 1990 the Committee for the Nobel Prizes announced that the 1990 Nobel Peace Prize would be awarded to Mikhail Gorbachev. The committee stated:

> During the last few years, dramatic changes have taken place in the relationship between East and West. Confrontation has been replaced by negotiations. Old European nation-states have regained their freedom. The arms race is slowing down. . . .
>
> These historic changes spring from several factors, but in 1990 the Nobel Committee wants to honor Mikhail Gorbachev for his many and decisive contributions.

GORBACHEV INTENDED TO GO TO OSLO IN DECEMBER TO ACCEPT the prize, but developments at home forced him to postpone the trip. His two major problems, the economy and the nationalities problem, merged. The newly elected non-Communist officials in many republics had run on platforms of greater freedom from Moscow's control. As shortages grew and prices rose, these leaders said forcefully that the huge Communist bureaucracy at the center of the nation was not providing for the needs of the republics, although it was spending huge quantities of their tax money. The long-standing arrangement of power flowing from the top down to the localities, through the levels of the Communist party, had been based on a one-party nation that no longer existed. It was time, said these leaders, to carry out what Gorbachev had proposed when he first came to power: reduce drastically the bureaucracy at the center. Boris Yeltsin made a specific proposal that his Russian republic reduce its contribution to the central government from 119 billion rubles in 1990 to 24 billion in 1991. That republic, with three fourths of the land in the Soviet Union and 51 percent of the people, would be better off if it were an independent nation. In Ukraine, the second largest republic, with the nation's best farmland, people also spoke of independence. Such talk made the hard-liners more determined than ever to maintain their power by whatever means necessary.

Gorbachev could see that such developments were logical results of *glasnost, perestroika,* and *demokratizatsiya,* the ideas he had introduced. But he still hoped it was possible to save both the Communist party and the Soviet Union. Still trying to keep the support of both the hard-liners and the democrats, he asked the parliament for some emergency powers to stop what seemed to be a decline into chaos, and he also began to talk with the democrats about a new form of union of the republics. In this new "federation," many present functions of the central government would be handled by the republics.

In Lithuania, where talk of independence was strongest, there were a number of citizens who had moved there from the Russian republic and whose nationality was Russian, not Lithuanian. One of the hard-liners got authorization from Gorbachev to "protect the rights of this minority." He then used that authority to seize by force the Lithuanian broadcasting center, a major source of ideas of independence. Fourteen civilians died defending the center. A week later five more died in Latvia in a similar operation.

Gorbachev was dismayed by the deaths. He decided to put the idea of a new form of union before the people in a nationwide referendum, held on March 17, 1991. The question on the ballot read: "Do you consider it necessary to preserve the Union of Soviet Socialist Republics as a renewed federation of equal sovereign republics, in which rights and freedoms of people of any nationality will be fully guaranteed?"

Slightly more than half of the citizens who voted supported Gorbachev by voting yes for preserving the union as a federation. But in six of the fifteen republics—the three Baltic states plus Armenia, Georgia, and Moldavia—advocates of complete independence urged voters to boycott the referendum. Gorbachev worked with the presidents of the other nine republics to draw up a treaty for a new union. They set August 20, 1991, as the day for the treaty to be signed. Gorbachev then went to a Black Sea resort for a short vacation before the signing.

The hard-liners saw in the new union the end of their power. Two days before the treaty was to be signed eight hard-liners in high positions tried to seize control of the government and oust Gorbachev. They cut Gorbachev's telephone lines, put him and his family under house arrest, and ordered him to resign. Gorbachev simply refused. The eight announced anyway that he was ill and unable to work, and that the vice

---

OVERLEAF:
*Boris Yeltsin, atop a tank in Moscow, calls on all citizens to resist
the August 1991 coup.*
Sovfoto/Eastfoto

president (who was one of the eight) was assuming the duties of the president.

Western newspapers called the attempt by the French term *coup*. Soviet newspapers used the German term *putsch,* and called its leaders simply "the eight." World history is full of such attempts, many of them successful. But this August coup failed entirely.

A major reason for the failure was the decisive action of Boris Yeltsin. The hard-liners had neglected to arrest him or to cut off his communications. As soon as he heard of the coup attempt he went to the headquarters of his government of the Russian republic. Too late, the eight sent tanks and troops to surround those headquarters. Yeltsin climbed onto one of the tanks, announced that he was taking command of all army and security forces in the Russian republic, and called on all citizens to resist the coup. It was the sort of dramatic gesture that had won him his elections. Many of the tank commanders turned their gun turrets around to defend rather than attack the headquarters. Tens of thousands of people gathered in and around the building to support Yeltsin. Most of them were young. Many were veterans of the war in Afghanistan. Many were youths until now apathetic about politics. Yeltsin had the personal magnetism to rally them, once the coup attempt had given them a cause to fight for.

The eight went on television to announce they were ruling the nation. It was obvious their hands were shaking as they spoke. Nowhere could they find forces to support the coup. Three days after they arrested Gorbachev, Yeltsin announced their attempt was ended. One of the eight committed suicide. That brought the death toll in the coup to four. Two men had been crushed by armored vehicles and one had been shot while trying to stop a tank. That was four too many deaths, but the number, compared to the millions who died in Lenin's revolution, showed how far the nation had progressed toward orderly processes of change.

Gorbachev returned to Moscow, a changed man to a changed city. The Communist party he had supported against such odds had nourished the eight who had betrayed him and the government, and other party officials had done nothing to resist them. Boris Yeltsin, longtime critic of the party, had saved the day and so had become the most powerful man in Moscow. Fortunately Yeltsin was wise enough to share power with Gorbachev while they considered the next steps for the nation.

Gorbachev resigned as head of the Communist party and then banned all its activities. Across the nation, party offices were padlocked until it was decided what to do with the party's many assets. Gorbachev, Yeltsin, and the presidents of nine other republics formed a State Council to govern temporarily. One of the council's first actions was to recognize the independence of the three Baltic republics.

By December 1991 it was clear that any form of union, no matter how loosely bound together, would not satisfy the republics' demands for independence. Yeltsin met with the presidents of Ukraine and Byelorussia and formed a Commonwealth of Independent States with no ties to the Soviet government. The seven other republics represented in the State Council quickly joined the commonwealth, as did Armenia, making eleven members. Only the Georgian republic stayed out.

The Soviet Union had ceased to exist. Yeltsin claimed many items that had belonged to it for the newly independent Russian state, including membership in the Security Council of the United Nations and control of existing nuclear weapons. On Christmas night, December 25, 1991, Mikhail Gorbachev, president of a government without a country, announced his resignation from that post also. The flag of the USSR was taken down all over the land and replaced by the flags of the eleven independent states.

Sleds like this three-horse troika were the fastest and safest transportation on Russia's frozen winter highways.
Library of Congress

GLOSSARY

boyar. A Russian nobleman of high rank.

cossack. A frontiersman in czarist Russia who settled new lands, often by conquering the local inhabitants. Cossacks, known for their horsemanship, fighting skill, and independent spirit, sometimes served the czar in elite regiments, sometimes joined rebellions against him.

czar. The title of the Russian monarch, derived from the Roman *Caesar*. Also spelled tzar and tsar.

Duma. An assembly in czarist Russia with varying powers, from advising the ruler to drafting laws.

KGB Committee for National Security, a branch of the Soviet government with broad responsibilities, including espionage abroad and punishment of subversive activities at home. Successor to the czarist secret police; the Cheka; the NKVD; and the MVD.

kulak. Literally, "a tightfisted one," a farmer who accumulated wealth, ignoring Communist principles of equality.

Politburo. Political Bureau, the policy-making committee of the Communist party of the Soviet Union.

Russia. The empire of the czars. Also, the largest of the fifteen republics of the Union of Soviet Socialist Republics and the largest state of the Commonwealth of Independent States.

serf. A person required to live on a certain piece of land. In practice, a serf was required to till that land and give a part of the crop to the landowner.

show trials. Trials with verdicts set in advance, staged by Stalin to give an appearance of legality to his executions of those who opposed him.

soviet. Literally, a council. The government of the Union of Soviet Socialist Republics included soviets at many levels. Also, a citizen of the USSR.

streltsy. The elite regiments of guards responsible for defending Moscow until Peter the Great disbanded them.

Spellings. The Russian language uses the Cyrillic alphabet. For surnames and place names, this book uses the spellings given in *Webster's Ninth New Collegiate Dictionary, Webster's New Biographical Dictionary, and Webster's New Geographical Dictionary,* and for persons recently gaining prominence, the spellings used by the *New York Times.* For first names, English equivalents are used when those versions are long established in English-speaking countries, e.g., Peter Tchaikovsky and Czar Nicholas.

Dates. When the other nations of Europe corrected the calendar in 1752, Russia did not. As a result, dates in Russia were eleven, then twelve, then thirteen days behind, until Lenin reset the calendar on February 1, 1918, making it February 14. Because events such as the October Revolution are named by the old calendar, old dates are used in this book up to 1918.

BIBLIOGRAPHY

BETHELL, NICHOLAS. *Russia Besieged*. Alexandria, Va.: Time-Life Books, 1977.

BILLINGTON, JAMES H. *The Icon and the Axe: An Interpretive History of Russian Culture*. New York: Alfred A. Knopf, 1967.

CRONIN, VINCENT. *Catherine, Empress of All the Russias*. New York: William Morrow, 1978.

DMYTRYSHYN, BASIL. *USSR: A Concise History*. 4th edition. New York: Charles Scribner's Sons, 1984.

DODER, DUSKO, AND LOUISE BRANSON. *Gorbachev: Heretic in the Kremlin*. New York: Viking, 1990.

EDITORS OF TIME-LIFE BOOKS. *The Soviet Union*. Alexandria, Va.: Time-Life Books, 1977.

FLORINSKY, MICHAEL T. *Russia: A Short History*. 2d edition. London: Macmillan, 1969.

FRONCEK, THOMAS, ED. *The Horizon Book of the Arts of Russia*. New York: American Heritage, 1970.

GALE, ROBERT P., AND THOMAS HAUSER. *Final Warning: The Legacy of Chernobyl*. New York: Warner Books, 1989.

GORBACHEV, MIKHAIL. *The August Coup: The Truth and the Lessons*. New York: HarperCollins, 1991.

———. *Perestroika: New Thinking for Our Country and the World*. New York: Harper and Row, 1987.

GRAY, FRANCINE DUPLESSIS. *Walking the Tightrope: Lives of Soviet Women*. New York: Doubleday, 1990.

GREY, IAN. *The Horizon History of Russia.* New York: American Heritage, 1970.

GRULIOW, LEO. *Moscow.* Alexandria, Va.: Time-Life Books, 1977.

HELLER, MIKHAIL, AND ALEXANDER NEKRICH. *Utopia in Power: The History of the Soviet Union from 1917 to the Present.* Translated by Phyllis B. Carlos. New York: Summit Books, 1986.

KENNAN, GEORGE F. *Memoirs: 1925–1950.* Boston: Little, Brown, 1967.

KERBLAY, BASILE. *Gorbachev's Russia.* Translated by Rupert Swyer. New York: Pantheon Books, 1989.

KHRUSHCHEV, NIKITA. *The Last Testament.* Vol. 2 of *Khrushchev Remembers.* Translated and edited by Strobe Talbott. Boston: Little, Brown, 1974.

LAWRENCE, LOUISE DEKIRILINE. *Another Winter, Another Spring: A Love Remembered.* New York: McGraw-Hill, 1977.

LYONS, MERVIN. *Russia in Original Photographs 1860–1920.* Edited by Andrew Wheatcroft. New York: Charles Scribner's Sons, 1977.

MACLEAN, FITZROY. *Holy Russia: An Historical Companion to European Russia.* New York: Atheneum, 1979.

MASSIE, ROBERT K. *Nicholas and Alexandra.* New York: Atheneum, 1968.

———. *Peter the Great: His Life and World.* New York: Alfred A. Knopf, 1980.

MASSIE, SUZANNE. *Land of the Firebird: The Beauty of Old Russia.* New York: Simon and Schuster, 1980.

OBERG, JAMES E. *Red Star in Orbit.* New York: Random House, 1981.

PARES, BERNARD. *A History of Russia.* 5th edition. New York: Alfred A. Knopf, 1947.

PAYNE, ROBERT. *The Life and Death of Lenin.* New York: Simon and Schuster, 1964.

REED, JOHN. *Ten Days That Shook the World.* New York: Penguin Books, 1977.

SALISBURY, HARRISON. *Russia in Revolution: 1900–1930.* New York: Holt, Rinehart and Winston, 1978.

SHEPHERD, JACK. *Cannibals of the Heart: A Personal Biography of Louisa Catherine and John Quincy Adams.* New York: McGraw-Hill, 1980.

SMOLAN, RICK, AND DAVID COHEN, project directors. *A Day in the Life of the Soviet Union.* New York: Collins, 1987.

TRAVER, NANCY. *Kife: The Lives and Dreams of Soviet Youth.* New York: St. Martin's Press, 1989.

ULAM, ADAM B. *Stalin: The Man and His Era.* New York: Viking, 1973.

USTINOV, PETER. *My Russia.* Boston: Little, Brown, 1983.

VERNADSKY, GEORGE. *A History of Russia.* 6th edition. New Haven, Conn.: Yale University Press, 1969.

WALLACE, ROBERT. *Rise of Russia.* New York: Time, 1967.

WALSH, WARREN BARTLETT. *Russia and the Soviet Union: A Modern History.* Ann Arbor: University of Michigan Press, 1958.

INDEX